Slavery and Human Trafficking

Other Books of Related Interest:

Opposing Viewpoints Series

American Values

America's Prisons

Civil Liberties

Ethics

Illegal Immigration

At Issue Series

Age of Consent

Child Labor and Sweatshops

Guns and Crime

Minorities and the Law

Should the US Close Its Borders?

Current Controversies Series

Gangs

Immigration

Poverty and Homelessness

"Congress shall make no law . . . abridging the freedom of speech, or of the press."

First Amendment to the US Constitution

The basic foundation of our democracy is the First Amendment guarantee of freedom of expression. The Opposing Viewpoints series is dedicated to the concept of this basic freedom and the idea that it is more important to practice it than to enshrine it.

Slavery and Human Trafficking

Noah Berlatsky, Book Editor

GREENHAVEN PRESS
A part of Gale, Cengage Learning

Farmington Hills, Mich • San Francisco • New York • Waterville, Maine
Meriden, Conn • Mason, Ohio • Chicago

Judy Galens, *Manager, Frontlist Acquisitions*

For more information, contact:
Greenhaven Press
27500 Drake Rd.
Farmington Hills, MI 48331-3535
Or you can visit our Internet site at gale.cengage.com

Articles in Greenhaven Press anthologies are often edited for length to meet page requirements. In addition, original titles of these works are changed to clearly present the main thesis and to explicitly indicate the author's opinion. Every effort is made to ensure that Greenhaven Press accurately reflects the original intent of the authors. Every effort has been made to trace the owners of copyrighted material.

LIBRARY OF CONGRESS CATALOGING-IN-PUBLICATION DATA

Names: Berlatsky, Noah, editor.
Title: Slavery and human trafficking / Noah Berlatsky, Book Editor.
Description: Farmington Hills, Mich. : Greenhaven Press, 2016. | Series: Opposing viewpoints | Includes bibliographical references and index.
Identifiers: LCCN 2015027190 | ISBN 9780737775303 (hardcover) | ISBN 9780737775310 (pbk.)
Subjects: LCSH: Slavery--History--Juvenile literature. | Human trafficking--Juvenile literature. | Emigration and immigration--Government policy--Juvenile literature.
Classification: LCC HT861 .S375 2016 | DDC 364.15/51--dc23
LC record available at http://lccn.loc.gov/2015027190

Printed in the United States of America
1 2 3 4 5 20 19 18 17 16

Contents

Chapter 4: How Does Immigration Policy Affect Human Trafficking?

Why Consider Opposing Viewpoints?

> *"The only way in which a human being can make some approach to knowing the whole of a subject is by hearing what can be said about it by persons of every variety of opinion and studying all modes in which it can be looked at by every character of mind. No wise man ever acquired his wisdom in any mode but this."*
>
> *John Stuart Mill*

In our media-intensive culture it is not difficult to find differing opinions. Thousands of newspapers and magazines and dozens of radio and television talk shows resound with differing points of view. The difficulty lies in deciding which opinion to agree with and which "experts" seem the most credible. The more inundated we become with differing opinions and claims, the more essential it is to hone critical reading and thinking skills to evaluate these ideas. Opposing Viewpoints books address this problem directly by presenting stimulating debates that can be used to enhance and teach these skills. The varied opinions contained in each book examine many different aspects of a single issue. While examining these conveniently edited opposing views, readers can develop critical thinking skills such as the ability to compare and contrast authors' credibility, facts, argumentation styles, use of persuasive techniques, and other stylistic tools. In short, the Opposing Viewpoints Series is an ideal way to attain the higher-level thinking and reading skills so essential in a culture of diverse and contradictory opinions.

In addition to providing a tool for critical thinking, Opposing Viewpoints books challenge readers to question their own strongly held opinions and assumptions. Most people form their opinions on the basis of upbringing, peer pressure, and personal, cultural, or professional bias. By reading carefully balanced opposing views, readers must directly confront new ideas as well as the opinions of those with whom they disagree. This is not to argue simplistically that everyone who reads opposing views will—or should—change his or her opinion. Instead, the series enhances readers' understanding of their own views by encouraging confrontation with opposing ideas. Careful examination of others' views can lead to the readers' understanding of the logical inconsistencies in their own opinions, perspective on why they hold an opinion, and the consideration of the possibility that their opinion requires further evaluation.

Evaluating Other Opinions

To ensure that this type of examination occurs, Opposing Viewpoints books present all types of opinions. Prominent spokespeople on different sides of each issue as well as well-known professionals from many disciplines challenge the reader. An additional goal of the series is to provide a forum for other, less known, or even unpopular viewpoints. The opinion of an ordinary person who has had to make the decision to cut off life support from a terminally ill relative, for example, may be just as valuable and provide just as much insight as a medical ethicist's professional opinion. The editors have two additional purposes in including these less known views. One, the editors encourage readers to respect others' opinions—even when not enhanced by professional credibility. It is only by reading or listening to and objectively evaluating others' ideas that one can determine whether they are worthy of consideration. Two, the inclusion of such viewpoints encourages the important critical thinking skill of objectively evaluating an author's credentials and bias. This evaluation will illuminate an author's reasons for taking a particular stance on an issue and will aid in readers' evaluation of the author's ideas.

It is our hope that these books will give readers a deeper understanding of the issues debated and an appreciation of the complexity of even seemingly simple issues when good and honest people disagree. This awareness is particularly important in a democratic society such as ours in which people enter into public debate to determine the common good. Those with whom one disagrees should not be regarded as enemies but rather as people whose views deserve careful examination and may shed light on one's own.

Thomas Jefferson once said that "difference of opinion leads to inquiry, and inquiry to truth." Jefferson, a broadly educated man, argued that "if a nation expects to be ignorant and free . . . it expects what never was and never will be." As individuals and as a nation, it is imperative that we consider the opinions of others and examine them with skill and discernment. The Opposing Viewpoints series is intended to help readers achieve this goal.

David L. Bender and Bruno Leone,
Founders

Introduction

> *"Recruited as an inexpensive source of labor, enslaved Africans in the United States also became important economic and political capital in the American political economy. Enslaved Africans were legally a form of property—a commodity. Individually and collectively, they were frequently used as collateral in all kinds of business transactions. They were also traded for other kinds of goods and services."*
>
> *—Howard Dodson,*
> *"How Slavery Helped Build a World Economy,"*
> National Geographic,
> *February 3, 2003*

The reason for slavery seems clear enough. If you are a businessperson, one of your biggest expenses is labor. You have an incentive to pay workers as little as possible to keep profits for yourself. If you can enslave the workers, and pay them nothing at all, then you'll make more money than ever.

That makes sense in theory. But does it hold in practice? After all, keeping people in slavery can be expensive; one needs to police them constantly and hold them against their will. And will they do as good a job if they are enslaved as if they were not? Maybe the costs of enslaving people, from a purely economic standpoint, outweigh the benefits.

Historians have debated this issue for many years, especially in the context of slavery in the Southern United States before the Civil War. One common argument has been that while slavery may have had short-term economic benefits, it hurt the development of Southern capitalism in the long run.

For instance, the economist John Elliott Cairnes argued that since slaves did not really want to work, complicated, scientific methods of farming were difficult to implement. Soils were depleted more quickly, and new farming techniques were not adopted. Thus, Southern farms, Cairnes argued, were less competitive than their Northern rivals.

Historian Eugene Genovese added that slavery weakened the South because slaveholders did not have to seek profits. Slavery encouraged lavish displays of wealth. Slaveholders flaunted land and slaves rather than streamlining production and innovating new methods. Therefore, according to the *Economist* magazine, "rational economic decisions were sacrificed for pomp and circumstance."

Other historians, though, have suggested that slavery was in fact economically viable, and even innovative. Robert William Fogel and Stanley L. Engerman in their classic *Time on the Cross: The Economics of American Slavery* believed that slavery was very successful: "generally a highly profitable investment which yielded rates of return that compared favourably with the most outstanding investment opportunities in manufacturing." Given slavery's success, Fogel and Engerman believed that slaves were fairly well treated by planters who did not want to harm their good investment.

Edward E. Baptist in his 2014 book *The Half Has Never Been Told: Slavery and the Making of American Capitalism* agrees that slavery was lucrative—but not that slaves were well treated. Baptist points out that cotton production in the South grew by leaps and bounds throughout the pre–Civil War period. This was in part due to mechanical innovations, such as the cotton gin, which cleaned cotton more quickly. Cotton was still picked by hand, however, and the production increase meant that the picking was going faster and faster. Black slaves were figuring out ways to pick cotton ever more quickly. They had no financial incentive to do that. So why did they?

Baptist says that they picked faster and faster because Southern planters figured out new and horrible ways to torture them. The whip was used, but also "carpenters' tools, chains, cotton presses, hackles, handsaws, hoe handles, iron or branding livestock, nails, pokers, smoothing irons, singletrees, steelyards, tongs . . . every product sold in New Orleans stores converted into an instrument of torture," Baptist writes. This torture was applied carefully; slaves had to pick the same amount of cotton they had picked the day before, or more, every day, or face whipping and punishment. Torture, Baptist says, created the incentive to pick more and more—resulting in an incredibly efficient production chain, built on blood and pain. Southern success formed the basis for American wealth, and for America's superpower status. America's position in the world, Baptist concludes, is based on the economic triumph of slavery and torture.

Slavery as an organized economic system in the American South is gone now. However, slavery in various forms still persists. This is perhaps another piece of evidence that slavery is, and remains, profitable. Slavery today is estimated by the International Labour Organization to be a $32 billion a year business.

Opposing Viewpoints: Slavery and Human Trafficking examines issues of human exploitation in chapters titled "What Are Issues Surrounding Contemporary Slavery?," "Is Sex Trafficking a Serious Problem?," "How Does Legal Policy Toward Sex Work Affect Sex Trafficking?," and "How Does Immigration Policy Affect Human Trafficking?" The book points out various groups in many parts of the world who work under a slavery system because the people who run businesses find slavery profitable. If slavery were truly inefficient economically, it would presumably die out of its own accord. That has not happened yet and does not seem likely to happen in the near future.

What Are Issues Surrounding Contemporary Slavery?

Chapter Preface

Slavery is often seen as a historical issue; an evil that was ended with the American Civil War. However, slavery still exists throughout the world. Most slavery now is illegal and underground. One country, however, still employs slavery as government policy; that country is North Korea.

North Korea is a totalitarian country, and it allows little contact with the outside world. Still, it has long been known that the regime maintains vast prison camps in which torture, starvation, rape, and murder are commonplace. Up to two hundred thousand people may be held in these camps, according to human rights organization Amnesty International. According to Paul Armstrong in a 2013 report for CNN, one camp covers an area three times as large as Washington, DC. People are thrown in the camps for minor infractions, such as watching foreign soap operas or having a relative who is a political dissident. When children are born in the camps, they are often kept there, never allowed to see the outside.

People in the camps are forced to work and are essentially treated as slaves. For example, Amnesty International said that North Korea enclosed the Choma-Bong valley with guard towers and perimeters, essentially turning the whole area into a prison. Roseanne Rife, Amnesty International's East Asia chief, explained, "they've increased the workforce in the mines. And, the fact that they're enclosed in this perimeter then raises concerns about are they being forced to work in the mines as additional forced labor? And, what we normally see, the forced labor is very slave-like conditions."

In addition to the labor camps, North Korea has also trafficked its own citizens for slave labor. Since the 1980s, the North Korean regime has shipped workers abroad—most often to Russia and the Middle East. The numbers have risen in recent years; now as many as one hundred thousand North

Koreans may be sent into slavery abroad. Workers labor in sweatshop conditions, and their pay is sent back to the North Korean government. A Korean worker in Russia reported in the *Telegraph* in 2015, "There is no contract, they say they will give us health insurance and heating access but we never receive anything. In reality we earn about 300 rubles but they end up taking it all away."

The following chapter discusses aspects of contemporary slavery, including places where humans face exploitation and the question of whether US prisons are centers of slave labor.

VIEWPOINT 1

"Under kafala *it is impossible for a migrant worker domestic servant to find work elsewhere when her employer physically abuses her, as is it equally impossible for a migrant construction worker to find alternative work when his employer forces him to work 12 hours per day in 100 degree weather."*

Domestic Workers in Bahrain Face Trafficking and Exploitation

Americans for Democracy and Human Rights in Bahrain

Americans for Democracy and Human Rights in Bahrain (ADHRB) is an organization that works to foster democracy and human rights in Bahrain and the Middle East. In the following viewpoint, ADHRB reports that forced labor of migrant workers is a serious problem in Bahrain, Saudi Arabia, and Qatar. The kafala *system makes it illegal for migrant workers to change employers without permission. This creates exploitive situations in which workers who are sexually abused or kept in inhumane*

ADHRB, "Slaving Away: Migrant Labor Exploitation and Human Trafficking in the Gulf," adhrb.org, June 17, 2014.

working conditions cannot change jobs. ADHRB recommends that the governments of these nations enforce their laws against the kafala *system and move forward quickly to end the slavery of migrant workers.*

As you read, consider the following questions:

1. What have Qatar, Bahrain, and Saudi Arabia done to regulate the *kafala* system, and why does ADHRB say this is not sufficient?
2. Besides the *kafala* system, what are some of the other abuses that ADHRB discusses?
3. What specific policies in regard to slavery in Bahrain, Qatar, and Saudi Arabia does ADHRB recommend to the United States?

Since the creation of the modern metric for human rights standards, the member states of the Gulf Cooperation Council (GCC) have habitually ranked near the bottom. Yet, while the human rights situation of domestic persons in Gulf countries is very rightfully highlighted by both the international community and domestic civil society in their respective countries, the plight of migrant or trafficked workers in the Gulf is often understated by those same actors. "Slaving Away: Migrant Labor Exploitation and Human Trafficking in the Gulf" aims to fill that gap, analyzing the situation of migrant workers and human trafficking in three key Gulf countries: Bahrain, Qatar, and Saudi Arabia. In so doing, it examines not only promises and commitments made by the countries in regard to how they will tackle the enormous issues associated with migrants' rights, but also measures the implementation of those promises. It is not enough for a country to pass a law protecting migrant workers or criminalizing human trafficking; that law must be enforced in order for those protections to mean something.

The *Kafala* System

Central to this analysis is the issue of the *kafala* system, an oppressive employment system that quashes worker mobility by forcing migrant workers to continue their employment relationship with abusive employers. Ostensibly dismantled in Bahrain and with Qatar and Saudi Arabia having in the past made commitments towards at least weakening the system if not abolishing it completely, it is somewhat surprising that the *kafala* system continues to flourish in all three countries. In Qatar and Saudi Arabia, it is altogether illegal for an employee to seek alternative employment without first obtaining permission from his original employer, while in neighboring Bahrain a worker must wait a year before seeking permission from the government to relocate (a request that is routinely denied). This raises significant concerns, as under *kafala* it is impossible for a migrant worker domestic servant to find work elsewhere when her employer physically abuses her, as is it equally impossible for a migrant construction worker to find alternative work when his employer forces him to work 12 hours per day in 100 degree weather.

This is to say nothing of the litany of other abuses endemic for migrant workers in the Gulf. Promised a decent wage upon leaving their home country and hoping to send the extra back home, migrant workers often find themselves given wages at a less-than-subsistence level, or can even have their wages completely withheld for up to years at a time. Many migrant workers are forced into overcrowded and unsanitary labor camps lacking clean water or decent food. Oftentimes, young women are lured to Bahrain, Qatar, or Saudi Arabia with the promise of a well-paying domestic worker job for a good family, only to find themselves sold into sex slavery upon arrival. Runaways are labeled illegal, and can be detained for years or deported at their own expense as GCC governments effectively sponsor human rights violations.

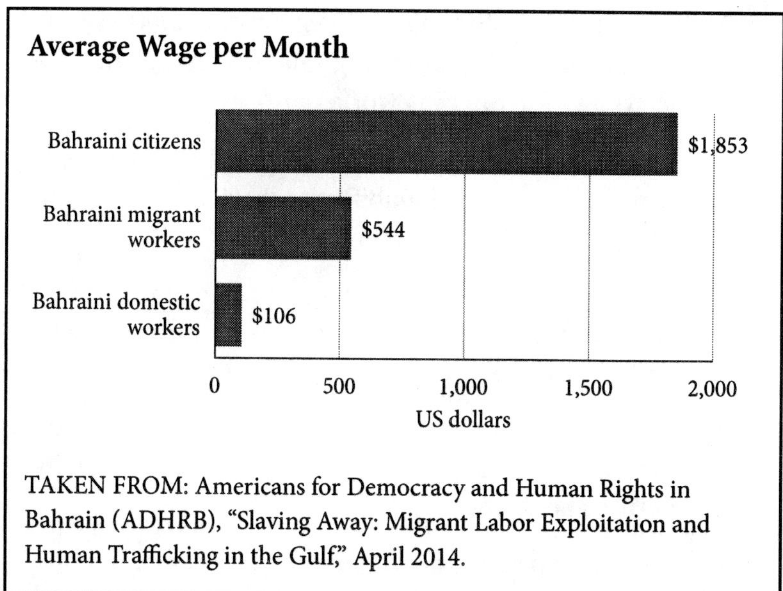

TAKEN FROM: Americans for Democracy and Human Rights in Bahrain (ADHRB), "Slaving Away: Migrant Labor Exploitation and Human Trafficking in the Gulf," April 2014.

Correcting these issues should be of paramount importance to the governments of Bahrain, Qatar, and Saudi Arabia, but so far efforts towards reform have been lackluster. The three countries have all individually legislated reform, but, as with so many other human rights commitments made by the three governments, progress towards implementation has been slow. With the plight of migrant workers in the Gulf now highlighted by the 2022 Qatar World Cup [referring to the FIFA World Cup being held in Qatar in 2022], however, migrant source countries as well as members of the international community have a renewed opportunity to push for a better realization of the rights of migrant workers in these countries. This report aims to inform those actors.

Policy Recommendations

ADHRB recommends the following for Bahrain, Qatar, Saudi Arabia; the international community; and citizens of the world:

To the Gulf Authorities:

1. With the goal of ultimately abolishing the *kafala* sponsorship system and establishing a new, fair, and justiciable system for migrant workers:
    1. Create and enforce a legal framework by which migrant workers have the ability to leave employers and seek alternative employment at will;
    2. Coordinate with governments of source countries to abolish exploitative and predatory recruitment agencies and systems;
    3. Develop and implement legislation criminalizing the physical abuse of migrant workers and the withholding of wages; [and]
    4. Establish expedient procedures for migrant complaints.
2. Introduce and enforce labor laws specifically for migrant workers that comply with international standards of fair labor practice and safe working conditions:
    1. Ensure that workers have access to adequate food and drinking water;
    2. Establish and enforce inspections of migrants' living camps to ensure decent and sanitary living environments;
    3. Ensure that physical laborers have access to necessary safety equipment;
    4. Generate and implement legislation providing maximum working hours and shifts, and ensure that employers will provide overtime payment for additional hours; [and]
    5. Coordinate with employers to ensure the use of health insurance, and establish compensation system for workers who sustain a permanent disability at work.

3. Effectively eliminate all child labor, forced labor, forced prostitution and human trafficking practices in the region:
    1. Coordinate with source countries to better identify, target, and dismantle human trafficking organizations;
    2. Create and implement legislation criminalizing human trafficking, and aggressively pursue and prosecute human and sex traffickers;
    3. Develop and enforce systems to identify and protect victims of forced sex trafficking, and specifically decriminalize the act of forced prostitution; and
    4. Provide sexually abused persons/survivors of sexual abuse with dignity, and provide legal assistance to punish perpetrators.

To the Governments of Source Countries:

1. Work in partnership with the governments of Bahrain, Qatar, and Saudi Arabia to ensure that the rights of migrant workers are protected:
    1. Coordinate with local governments and law enforcement to abolish exploitative and predatory recruitment agencies and systems;
    2. Increase the scope of support provided by diplomatic missions in Bahrain, Qatar, and Saudi Arabia to migrant workers facing exploitation or abuse; [and]
    3. Negotiate and enforce bilateral agreements with Bahrain, Qatar, and Saudi Arabia establishing appropriate standards of treatment for migrant workers.
2. Ensure transparency and accountability by regularly and publicly reporting data concerning all migrant workers and trafficked persons; and

3. Empower citizens via training regarding their future employment, their rights, and how to seek help once in Bahrain, Qatar, and Saudi Arabia.

To the Government of the United States:

1. Continue to pressure the governments of Bahrain, Qatar, and Saudi Arabia to adopt and implement international labor standards and human trafficking laws:
    1. Through the context of the free trade agreement with Bahrain, ensure Bahraini labor law complies with applicable legal protections regarding migrant workers; [and]
    2. Ensure and support free labor practices for all labor contracted through U.S. government assets in Gulf countries.
2. Recognize the expanding nature of the human trafficking problem in the Gulf by downgrading Qatar to Tier 2.5 Watch List and Bahrain to Tier 3 in the next Trafficking in Persons report.

To the International Community:

1. Request that Bahrain, Qatar, and Saudi Arabia ratify and implement all relevant international treaties and conventions relating to migrant workers, including:
    1. The ILO [International Labour Organization] conventions for migrant workers, forced labor, etc.; and
    2. The UN [United Nations] International Convention on the Protection of the Rights of All Migrant Workers and Members of Their Families.
2. Raise awareness of the current situation for migrant workers in Qatar, especially as it relates to the upcoming 2022 World Cup; and

3. Encourage the governments of Bahrain, Qatar, and Saudi Arabia to allow the special rapporteurs on trafficking in persons and the human rights of migrants to visit and evaluate according to their mandates.

Viewpoint 2

> *"Human trafficking is a complex human rights issue, and this case demonstrates how male immigrants with visas can be victims and survivors of trafficking."*

Indian Immigrants Are Trafficked to Mississippi Shipyards

Southern Poverty Law Center

The Southern Poverty Law Center (SPLC) is a legal advocacy nonprofit that focuses on civil rights issues. In the following viewpoint, SPLC describes a successful lawsuit against Signal International, a marine services company that hired workers from India. Signal promised the workers green cards and lured them into paying large sums to come to work in the United States. When the workers arrived, there were no green cards, and the men were forced to labor under abusive working conditions. The workers could not quit or speak up for fear of being deported. SPLC says the case illustrates the way that men can be victims of human trafficking.

Southern Poverty Law Center, "Federal Jury in SPLC Case Awards $14 Million to Indian Guest Workers Victimized in Labor Trafficking Scheme by Signal International and Its Agents," splcenter.org, February 18, 2015.

As you read, consider the following questions:

1. For what jobs were the Indian men recruited, according to SPLC?
2. Why does SPLC say the men could not quit their jobs?
3. According to SPLC, what did the workers do that caused Signal to try to retaliate against them?

A federal jury in an SPLC [Southern Poverty Law Center] case today awarded $14 million in compensatory and punitive damages to five Indian guest workers who were defrauded and exploited in a labor trafficking scheme engineered by a Gulf Coast marine services company, an immigration lawyer and an Indian labor recruiter who lured hundreds of workers to a Mississippi shipyard with false promises of permanent U.S. residency.

Post-Katrina Scam

After a four-week trial before U.S. District Judge Susie Morgan, the jury ruled that Signal International, New Orleans lawyer Malvern C. Burnett and India-based recruiter Sachin Dewan engaged in labor trafficking, fraud, racketeering and discrimination. The jury also found that one of the five plaintiffs was a victim of false imprisonment and retaliation.

"The defendants exploited our clients, put their own profits over the lives of these honorable workers, and tried to deny them their day in court," said lead attorney Alan Howard, Southern Poverty Law Center board chairman and a partner in Crowell & Moring's New York office. "But they persevered and after seven long years have received the justice they so well deserve."

The trial was the first in a series of cases spearheaded by the SPLC that together comprise one of the largest labor trafficking cases in U.S. history.

"This historic verdict puts American companies on notice that if they exploit the flaws in our temporary worker program, they will be held accountable and punished," said Chandra Bhatnagar, co-counsel in the case and senior staff attorney with the American Civil Liberties Union Human Rights Program. "In a victory for justice, the jury has reaffirmed the fundamental principle that all people are entitled to human rights no matter where they're from or what their race or immigration status is."

In the aftermath of Hurricane Katrina [which devastated New Orleans in 2005], Signal used the U.S. government's H-2B guest worker program to import nearly 500 men from India to work as welders, pipe fitters and in other positions to repair damaged oil rigs and related facilities.

The workers each paid the labor recruiters and a lawyer between $10,000 and $20,000 or more in recruitment fees and other costs after recruiters promised good jobs, green cards and permanent U.S. residency for them and their families. Most sold property or plunged their families deeply into debt to pay the fees.

When the men arrived at Signal shipyards in Pascagoula, Mississippi, beginning in 2006, they discovered that they wouldn't receive the green cards or permanent residency that had been promised. Signal also forced them each to pay $1,050 a month to live in isolated, guarded labor camps where as many as 24 men shared a space the size of a double-wide trailer. None of Signal's non-Indian workers were required to live in the company housing.

"That was the minute where all my expectations were shattered," plaintiff Sony Sulekha testified. "The time that I went into the camp and I looked, I was shocked. Where all my expectations and my happiness all got destroyed, that was the minute that it happened."

Under the guest worker program, workers are not allowed to change jobs if they are abused but face the loss of their investment if they are fired or quit.

$8 Million Scheme

An economist who reviewed Signal's records estimated the company saved more than $8 million in labor costs by hiring the Indian workers at below-market wages.

Together, the H-2B visa status, the high debt, the poor conditions at the labor camp and the discriminatory treatment and disparagement based on their race or nationality led the men to feel trapped. "These men experienced constant stress and humiliation," said Dan Werner, SPLC supervising attorney. "Yet, they were stuck. The defendants showed a shocking disregard for their basic human rights."

When some men tried to find their own housing, Signal officials told them the "man camp" fee would still be deducted from their pay. Visitors were rarely allowed into the camps. Company employees searched workers' belongings. And workers who complained were threatened with deportation—a disastrous prospect for those who mortgaged their futures to obtain the jobs.

"I had borrowed so much money to come here," Sulekha testified. "And then if I am returned [to India by Signal for standing up for my rights], then my entire family would [be in] the streets."

These abuses silenced plaintiff Andrews Issac Padavettiyil.

"Until today, I have not told anything to any other person about all of the difficulties that I had," he testified. "In the future, I don't want anybody to go through these same problems. I had to say Signal was a big part of this."

Retaliation

In March 2007, some of the SPLC's clients were illegally detained by Signal's private security guards during a predawn raid of their quarters in Pascagoula. Two were detained for the purpose of deporting them to India in retaliation for complaining about the abuses and meeting with workers' rights advocates. One worker who is a plaintiff in a separate suit was so distraught he attempted suicide.

After the treatment of these workers came to light, a 2008 Signal press release declared the company would take legal action and demand that lost earnings be returned to the guest workers. But during cross-examination, Signal CEO [chief executive officer] Richard L. Marler said that the company had not taken any legal action to return lost earnings to these workers. Signal had, however, taken legal action against others involved in the recruitment of these guest workers to compensate the company for the alleged damages it had suffered.

"Human trafficking is a complex human rights issue, and this case demonstrates how male immigrants with visas can be victims and survivors of trafficking," said Ivy O. Suriyopas, director of the Asian American Legal Defense and Education Fund's anti-trafficking initiative. "The jury understood this nuance and has helped these men to finally achieve some measure of justice."

The other lawsuits facing Signal International and its agents, representing more than 200 additional workers, were filed after a judge did not grant class-action status in this case, which would have allowed the suit to benefit most of Signal's guest workers. The SPLC coordinated an unprecedented legal collaboration that brought together nearly a dozen of the nation's top law firms and civil rights organizations to represent, on a pro bono basis, hundreds of workers excluded from the original SPLC suit by the denial of class-action status.

The SPLC's co-counsel in this case are Crowell & Moring, LLP, the American Civil Liberties Union, the Asian American Legal Defense and Education Fund, Sahn Ward Coschignano & Baker, and the Louisiana Justice Institute.

Viewpoint 3

"Prison labor is the new slave labor."

Prison Labor: Three Strikes and You're Hired

Caitlin Seandel

Caitlin Seandel is a recent graduate from the international security and conflict resolution and women's studies programs at San Diego State University, and she is a member of the Ella's Voice *editorial board. In the following viewpoint, she reports that prison labor is big business. Prisoners do a great deal of work, especially in producing equipment for US military contractors. Seandel says that prison working conditions are often unsafe and that prisoners are frequently coerced into working. She argues that prison labor is effectively forced labor and slavery and that reform is needed.*

As you read, consider the following questions:

1. What is UNICOR, according to the author?
2. According to Seandel, what are economic incentives for corporations to use prison labor?

3. According to Seandel, how many prisoners are there in the United States?

First, two facts:

- My 20-year-young cousin is currently a proud Marine serving in Afghanistan.
- The United States imprisons more people per capita than any other country.

What's the connection? Prisoners. Not prisoners of war but the people locked up in our domestic prisons and jails—and, more specifically, their labor.

Surprised? I sure was.

Prison Labor: Way More than License Plates

Whenever I think of prison labor, the first thing in my head is license plates. Turns out, prison labor has come a long way from its humble roots of license plates and linen. While these industries are still prevalent, they are not big breadwinners.

The industry that takes the cake when it comes to prison labor is military supplies.

It is estimated that the federal prison industry produces 100% of all military helmets, ID tags, bulletproof vests, canteens, night-vision goggles, ammunition belts, tents, shirts, bags and pants.

And what company is there to oversee production of all these items? UNICOR.

UNICOR was previously known as Federal Prison Industries, which is a for-profit organization, and the 39th largest US contractor.

UNICOR operates 110 factories at 79 federal penitentiaries and the Department of Defense is one of their largest contracts. In 2001, UNICOR sales were $583.5 million—about $388 million of which was to DOD, or 66.5% of all business.

Prison Labor Offers "Economic Incentives" for Corporations

With wages as low as $0.23 per hour and no unions, safety regulations, pension, Social Security, sick leave nor overtime, prison labor is a growing and economically competitive sector.

Prison labor is competitive with sweatshop labor prices and, since production is domestic, incurs lower shipping costs. Plus, overhead is pretty much paid for by US taxpayers!

With all these economic incentives, it's no surprise that 37 states have legalized the contracting of prison labor by private corporations who bring their operations inside prison walls.

While UNICOR is among the leaders in using prison labor, other companies are taking advantage of the contract opportunities, including Nordstrom, Eddie Bauer, Motorola, Microsoft, Victoria's Secret, Compaq, IBM, Boeing, AT&T, Texas Instruments, Revlon, Macy's, Target, Nortel, Hewlett-Packard, Intel, Honeywell, Pierre Cardin, 3com, and Lucent Technologies, among others.

The One Place Where Slavery Is Still Legal in the US

If all a business is looking at is cutting costs and maximizing profit, prison labor is a smart investment.

But at the Ella Baker Center, we like to ask what is the human cost of this so-called "smart investment?"

In this case, the situation is clear: *Prison labor is the new slave labor.*

This is especially true considering that under the 13th Amendment, slavery is still legal—in prisons.

There are clear parallels between the new and the old:

Prison Labor and Union Busting

What's so attractive about using prison labor is precisely that it undoes everything that union members—and their parents and grandparents before them—have fought so hard to achieve. At times, prisoners have been used directly as a strike-breaking workforce; TWA's [Trans World Airlines'] reservations system was set up during a flight attendant strike, and according to the union involved, the prisoner program was a significant part of the company's strategy to undermine the strike. In other cases, prisons have allowed employers to avoid unions even in well-organized industries; thus, the owners of an Arizona slaughterhouse shut down their unionized operation only to reopen in a joint venture with the state's Department of Corrections. Even where it is not directly related to anti-union strategies, however, prison labor provides employers a means of avoiding or undoing virtually all of the gains won by working people over the past hundred years—creating islands of time in which, in terms of labor relations, it's still the late nineteenth century.

Prison labor is, of course, much cheaper than free labor for employers. In Ohio, for example, a Honda supplier paid auto workers $2/hour for the same work that the UAW [United Automobile Workers] had fought for decades to win $20–30/hour for. And in Oregon, private companies can "lease" prisoners for $3/day.

Paul Wright, "Making Slave Labor Fly."
Prison Nation: the Warehousing of America's Poor.
Eds. Tara Herivel and Paul Wright.
New York: Routledge, 2003.

- *Atrocious working conditions*: As mentioned above, there are no workers' rights/protection. Many prisoners work with toxic materials and are not given the proper protective clothing. Workdays often run past eight hours, with no breaks.

- *Coercion*: Prisoners frequently lose "good-time" and canteen privileges if they refuse to work. Georgia had one of the largest inmate protests in US history after prisoners were forced to work seven days in a row without pay and were beaten if they did not comply.
- *Exporting of inmates*: With the high incarceration rate in the US and overcrowding considered cruel and unusual punishment, the private prison industry has flourished, offering states and counties "rent-a-cell" services, in which the county makes $1.50 per bed.
- *Racial inequality*: The US has more than 2.3 million prisoners. People of color make up just 30% of total US population, but account for 60% of those locked up. There are now more black men in prison, parole or probation than were enslaved in the 1850s.

Prisons in Service to Profit, Not Public Safety

The reality in the US today is that prison is not for rehabilitation, it is for profit. With that kind of mentality, we are living up to our nickname of the United States of Incarceration.

The idea of working while in prison could be a tool for rehabilitation and, ultimately, greater public safety, but as usual the execution of the idea is most important.

Humans have rights and prisoners are human, therefore, prisoners have rights and those rights need to implemented and protected.

What Can You Do?

Working for the rights of prisoners is an uphill battle and educating yourself is the first step. Here are some links:

- "The Prison Industry in the United States: Big Business or a New Form of Slavery?" by Vicky Peláez
- "Prison Labor: Workin' for the Man" by Reese Erlich
- "The Pentagon and Slave Labor in U.S. Prisons" by Sara Flounders
- UNICOR's menu of products and services available through prison labor

VIEWPOINT 4

"Purposelessness and excruciating boredom, not overwork, are the dominant feature of most prison yards."

US Prisons Are Not a Center of Slave Labor

James Kilgore

James Kilgore is a research scholar at the Center for African Studies at the University of Illinois at Urbana-Champaign. In the following viewpoint, he argues that prisoners are not often used for slave labor. Security concerns make it hard for corporations to operate in prisons, and prisons have in any case moved away from offering educational or work opportunities. Instead, most prisoners are simply warehoused with nothing to do. Even when they emerge from prison, they often are stigmatized and denied work opportunities. Kilgore concludes that the focus on slave labor in prisons distracts attention from larger problems, such as a need for social services and the stigma prisoners face when they look for work.

James Kilgore, "The Myth of Prison Slave Labor Camps in the U.S.," counterpunch.org, August 11, 2013.

As you read, consider the following questions:

1. How does Kilgore describe his own memories of six years in prison?
2. What sort of security issues can cause work to stop for hours or days, according to Kilgore?
3. What corporations does Kilgore say have had money from prisons?

As Adam Gopnik reminds us, "mass incarceration on a scale almost unexampled in human history is a fundamental fact of our country today—perhaps *the* fundamental fact, as slavery was the fundamental fact of 1850." The racialization of this process, popularized by author Michelle Alexander as *The New Jim Crow*, has meant that African Americans in the U.S. now have more than triple the incarceration rate of blacks in South Africa at the peak of apartheid.

A Popular Narrative

In the haste to impart some rationality to all this, many activists and analysts have been quick to point to corporations as the sole culprits behind the prison industrial complex (PIC). An important component of this perspective is the notion of prisons as "slave labor camps." In this scenario, a sea of multinational corporations super-exploit hundreds of thousands of contract prison laborers to heartlessly augment their bottom lines. Late last year [2012] researchers Steve Fraser and Joshua Freeman took up this point in a study that they presented in a *CounterPunch* article, arguing that "penitentiaries have become a niche market for such work. The privatization of prisons in recent years has meant the creation of a small army of workers too coerced and right-less to complain."

Their perspective has resonated with a number of news services, anti–mass incarceration blogsters and activists. For example, a recent report from Russian news service RT claimed that prisons are "becoming America's own Chinese-style manufacturing line." *Huffington Post* picked up the story, quoting Fraser and Freeman:

> "All told, nearly a million prisoners are now making office furniture, working in call centers, fabricating body armor, taking hotel reservations, working in slaughterhouses, or manufacturing textiles, shoes, and clothing, while getting paid somewhere between 93 cents and $4.73 per day."

The *HuffPost* went on to name Chevron, Bank of America, AT&T, Starbucks and Walmart as major participants in what they called a "competitive spiral" to capture prison labor at the lowest possible wage levels. Vicky Peláez, writing for Global Research earlier this year called prison industry a "new form of slavery" identifying more than twenty corporations involved in contract arrangements. Her list included IBM, Pierre Cardin, Target and Hewlett-Packard. She concluded that, "thanks to prison labor, the United States is once again an attractive location for investment in work that was designed for Third World labor markets."

Prison Slavery Is Not Typical

As appealing as these scenarios are to our sense of moral outrage and the role of multinational corporations as the villains of our era, such assertions about prison labor are off the mark. I spent six and a half years in federal and state prisons at high, medium and low security levels. In all these institutions, very few people, if any, were under contract to private corporations. My memories of prison yards feature hundreds and hundreds of men trying to pump some meaning into their life with exercise routines, academic study, compulsive sports betting, religious devotion, and a number of creative and entrepreneurial "hustles." But being under the thumb of Microsoft founder Bill Gates or entering a Nike sweatshop was just about the furthest thing from our warehoused reality.

Statistics bear my memories out. Virtually all private sector prison labor is regulated under the Prison Industry Enhancement Certification Program (PIECP). Any prison wanting to publicly market goods worth more than $10,000 must register with PIECP. The PIECP statistical report for the first quarter of 2012 showed 4,675 incarcerated people employed in prison or jail PIECP programs, a miniscule portion of the nation's more than two million behind bars.

Likely the largest single user of contract prison labor is Federal Prison Industries [also known as UNICOR], which handles such arrangements for the [Federal] Bureau of Prisons (BOP). Of the nearly 220,000 people housed in BOP facilities, just 13,369, representing approximately 8% of the work eligible "inmates" were employed as of September 30, 2012. However, the overwhelming majority of this production was for government departments like defense and homeland security, rather than private corporations.

Security Trumps Profits

There is an economic rationality to why prison labor is so infrequently used. While incarcerated people may constitute a captive workforce, in the era of mass incarceration, security trumps all other institutional needs, including production deadlines. A fight on the yard, a surprise cell search, even a missing tool can occasion a lockdown where all activities, including work assignments, come to a halt for hours, days, or, in some cases even weeks or months. Multinational corporations accustomed to just-in-time production systems and flexible working hours don't respond well to this type of rigidity.

Portraying our prisons as slave labor camps satisfies a certain emotional appeal, but hunting down multinationals that are extracting super-profits from the incarcerated diverts us from the crucial labor issues at the heart of mass incarceration. Those behind bars constitute a displaced and discarded labor force, marginalized from mainstream employment on the streets by deindustrialization in their communities and the gutting of urban education in poor communities of color. More than half of all black men without a high school diploma will go to prison at some time in their lives. The school to prison pipeline is far more of a reality than slave labor camps.

Plus, the shift of the prison system's emphasis from rehabilitation to punishment in the last three decades has blocked opportunities for people to upgrade skills and education while incarcerated. As the nuns used to tell me in grade school: "an idle mind is the devil's workshop and idle hands are the devil's tools." The brains behind our prison system clearly had the devil's welfare in mind when they reoriented our institutions away from rehabilitation into warehousing millions of people while stripping away their opportunities for personal and collective development. As a result, purposelessness and excruciating boredom, not overwork, are the dominant features of most prison yards.

For those trying to put an end to mass incarceration, framing the labor issues of the prison industrial complex in this way takes us down a very different road than upgrading the conditions of the minute numbers behind bars who are under corporate contracts (or as some unions are wont to do—portraying prison laborers as scabs who undermine hard-won working-class gains). The chief labor concerns about mass incarceration are linked to broader inequalities in the economy as a whole, particularly the lack of employment for poor youth of color and the proliferation of low-wage jobs with no benefits. Employment creation and the restoration of much-needed state-provided social services like substance abuse or mental health treatment are the measures that will keep people on the streets. Forget about minimum wages for the mythical millions working for Microsoft in Leavenworth and Attica.

Exclusion from the Workforce

But the labor aspect of mass incarceration doesn't end there. People with a felony conviction carry a stigma, a brand often accompanied by exclusion from the labor market. Michelle Alexander calls "felon" the new "N" word. Indeed in the job world, those of us with felony convictions face a number of unique barriers. The most well known is "the box"—that question on employment applications that asks about criminal background. Eleven states and more than 40 cities and counties have outlawed the box on employment applications. Supporters of "ban the box" argue that questions about previous convictions amount to a form of racial discrimination since such a disproportionate number of those with felony convictions are African American and Latino. Advancing these ban-the-box campaigns will have a far more important impact on incarcerated people as workers than pressing for higher wages for those under contract to big companies inside.

However, even without the box, the rights of the formerly incarcerated in the labor market remain heavily restricted. Many professions, trades and service occupations that require certification bar or limit the accreditation of people with felony convictions. For example, a study by the mayor of Chicago's office found that of 98 Illinois state statutes regarding professional licensing, 57 contained restrictions for applicants with a criminal history, impacting over 65 professions and occupations. In some instances, even people applying for licenses to become barbers or cosmetologists face legal impediments.

Those with felony convictions face further hurdles when trying to access state assistance to tide them over during times of unemployment. In most states, those with drug convictions are banned from access to SNAP (food stamps) for life. Many local public housing authorities bar people with felony convictions, even if their parents or partners already reside there.

Lastly, the very conditions of parole often create obstacles to employment. Many states require that an employer of a person on parole agree that the workplace premises can be searched at any time without prior warning—hardly an attractive proposition for any business. In addition, tens of thousands of people on parole are subject to house arrest with electronic monitors. All movement outside the house must be preapproved by their parole agent. This makes changes in work schedule or jobs that involve travel an enormous challenge. Some basic changes to the conditions of parole could constitute an important step to easing the labor market conditions for people coming home from prison trying to secure and keep a job.

All of this is not to deny that many corporations have made huge amounts of money from mass incarceration. Firms like Arizona's Kitchell construction, which has built more than 40 state prisons and 30 adult jails, have made millions. The Tennessee-based Bob Barker enterprises is a "household" name among the incarcerated. With a corporate vision of "transforming criminal justice by honoring God in all we do," Barker has reaped massive profits from producing the poorest quality consumer goods, including two-inch toothbrushes, for people behind bars. Then, of course, we have private prison operators like CCA [Corrections Corporation of America] and the GEO Group. Although the privates control only 8% of prison beds nationally, these two firms managed to bring in over 3 billion in revenue last year.

While such profiteering continues, the prison industrial complex remains driven by an agenda that is more about politics than profits. State-owned prisons and political agendas continue to lie at the center of mass incarceration. The combined revenue of CCA and the GEO Group for 2012 was less than half of the California state corrections budget. Politicians, with important influence from pro-corporate organizations like the American Legislative Exchange Council (ALEC), have made the PIC possible by passing harsh sentencing laws, funding the war on drugs, tightening immigration legislation, and creating isolation units. . . . They have built a base of popular support for the "color-blind" approach of "lock 'em up and throw away the key." So while we need to curb the opportunities for corporate profit from putting people in cages, the main target of any campaign against the PIC must be to counter the racist ideology of "punitive populism" and reverse the political processes that perpetuate mass incarceration and the criminalization of the poor.

Periodical and Internet Sources Bibliography

The following articles have been selected to supplement the diverse views presented in this chapter.

Diane Black — "'Modern Day Slavery': America Must Fight Epidemic of Human Trafficking Here at Home," FoxNews.com, May 19, 2014.

Erin Fuchs — "This Is What Modern-Day Sex Slavery in America Looks Like," Business Insider, August 11, 2014.

Alexander E.M. Hess and Thomas C. Frohlich — "Countries with the Most Enslaved People," *USA Today*, November 23, 2014.

Sophie Kleeman — "Modern-Day Slavery Still Exists—And It's Thriving Across America," Mic, October 23, 2014.

Nicholas Kristof — "Slavery Isn't a Thing of the Past," *New York Times*, November 6, 2013.

Jim Liske — "Yep, Slavery Is Still Legal," *USA Today*, August 14, 2014.

Vicky Pelaez — "The Prison Industry in the United States: Big Business or a New Form of Slavery?," Global Research, March 31, 2014.

Jeanne Sahadi — "Slave Labor in America Today," CNN, October 21, 2014.

Jennifer Turner — "US Admits Modern-Day Slavery Exists at Home," American Civil Liberties Union, June 24, 2014.

Ian Urbina — "Using Jailed Migrants as a Pool of Cheap Labor," *New York Times*, May 24, 2014.

Chapter 2

Is Sex Trafficking a Serious Problem?

Chapter Preface

Sex trafficking is usually discussed as crime directed specifically at women and girls. The truth, however, is that men and boys also can be victims of sexual exploitation and violence.

The International Labour Organization (ILO) says that 98 percent of the victims of sex trafficking are women. The other 2 percent are men and boys—though it is possible the numbers are higher, since male victims are especially unlikely to report that they have been trafficked. For example, a 2008 study found that boys made up about 50 percent of sexually exploited children in New York.

Even when men do come forward, almost no resources are available to help them. According to an article for the Human Trafficking Search website, in 2014 a survey found not one bed set aside for male minor victims of sex trafficking in the entire United States in residential treatment centers. Of forty-three organizations surveyed by Shared Hope International, not one directed services especially to male survivors. International organizations do somewhat better: The United Arab Emirates opened its first center for male victims of trafficking in 2015. Still, the population is severely underserved.

Since male trafficking victims are rarely discussed, it is no wonder that they are subject to stereotypes and are often misunderstood. Boys are often assumed to be strong enough to escape from slavery if they want to. They are also often thought to be gay. According to a 2014 article by Yu Sun Chin for the Juvenile Justice Information Exchange, "When people think about male prostitution, they think of it as gay phenomena, that [the boys] are in control of what they're doing," said Steven Procopio, a program coordinator at Surviving Our Struggle, an organization that works with male trafficking victims. "They don't see them as victims."

Not all trafficking victims are women and girls; similarly, not all pimps and johns are men. One study, cited by Jodie Gummow at the AlterNet site, found that most trafficked children were forced to provide sexual services to men twenty-five to fifty-five years of age. However, 40 percent of boys and 11 percent of girls had female clients, and 13 percent of boys served exclusively female clients. Traffickers themselves are 35 to 40 percent women, according to AlterNet. Female traffickers include women in trafficking organizations, but they also include mothers and family members who may force their own children to sell sex.

Myths and stereotypes about the gender of trafficking victims and traffickers can make it difficult to help those in need or to catch perpetrators and hold them to account. The following chapter examines issues surrounding sex trafficking.

Viewpoint 1

> *"This is a multimillion-dollar industry that affects every country in the world, including ours, cities and suburbs alike."*

Sex Trafficking Is a Worldwide Problem

Erin Weaver

In the following news article, The Reporter *indicates that human trafficking is a worldwide, multimillion-dollar industry. The article further points to a recent conviction of a man who led a prostitution ring as an example of human trafficking. According to* The Reporter, *women may be lured by promises of money or fame, only to realize that they cannot get out of the sex industry. The article concludes that increased awareness and more law enforcement can help reduce human trafficking.*

As you read, consider the following questions:

1. How many people does Weaver say are trafficked over the US border?

Erin Weaver, "Human Trafficking Not Just a Global Problem; Issue Impacts Montgomery, Bucks Counties," *The Reporter*, January 11, 2014.

2. According to the viewpoint, how does Dan Emr say women can be tricked into the sex industry?
3. What kinds of contemporary slavery does President Obama mention in the speech quoted by Weaver?

January is National Slavery and Human Trafficking Prevention Month, also referred to as Human Trafficking Awareness Month. How aware are you of human trafficking?

A Multimillion-Dollar Industry

Globally, there are millions of women and children enslaved in the human trafficking industry. According to the FBI's [Federal Bureau of Investigation's] 2011 report on trafficking, it is the fastest-growing business of organized crime and the third-largest criminal enterprise in the world.

There is a common misconception about human trafficking: that it takes place elsewhere in the world, not in the United States and definitely not in Montgomery County. But in fact, there are an estimated 293,000 American youths currently at risk of becoming victims of commercial sexual exploitation, according to the FBI report.

And there are between 600,000 and 800,000 people trafficked across the U.S. border—half of them are children, and 80 percent of them are female. Human trafficking is absolutely a global problem, but it is also a national—and local—problem.

That's according to U.S. Rep. Mike Fitzpatrick, R-8, who has been active in supporting House bills preventing and addressing human trafficking.

"I spoke with my staff a little over a year ago on this, after speaking with members of Congress who were also concerned about emerging statistics on an issue that we all felt, growing up, was an issue for a foreign country," Fitzpatrick said. "But the reality is that this is a multimillion-dollar industry that affects every country in the world, including ours, cities and suburbs alike, and that includes Philadelphia and the towns around it."

Prostitution in Montgomery County

And if you're looking for a case of sex trafficking in Montgomery County, consider Florencio Perez Martinez, a 45-year-old man from Perkiomen Township who just faced more than 100 felony and misdemeanor prostitution-related charges for allegedly running a five-county sex-trade business.

As of Dec. 19 [2013], Martinez, a Mexican national residing in the U.S. illegally, faces 11-and-a-half to 23 months in the county jail, then deportation.

"He was part of an enterprise that was running a prostitution business pretty much all over Montgomery County," said Assistant District Attorney Jordan Friter, who sought jail time against Martinez, according to Digital First Media [DFM] archives. "He would pick up a girl each week at a bus station, either in Norristown or Philadelphia, would house her for a week, drive her around to customers, collect the money from her and then take her back to the bus station and pick up a new girl."

Martinez had been operating his business since January 2011 as part of an organization supplying adult women to customers in Montgomery, Bucks, Philadelphia, Chester and Delaware Counties who paid for the women's sexual services. According to DFM archives, customers paid the women between $25 and $30 for sex; Martinez then took a $10 to $12 cut from the women.

"It's the kind of crime that affects a whole community. It was throughout Montgomery County. He was doing this right in quiet neighborhoods and this type of activity can't be tolerated by the community," said Friter, who leads the district attorney's sex crimes prosecution unit.

President Obama on Human Trafficking in the United States

But for all the progress that we've made, the bitter truth is that trafficking also goes on right here, in the United States. It's the migrant worker unable to pay off the debt to his trafficker. The man, lured here with the promise of a job, his documents then taken, and forced to work endless hours in a kitchen. The teenage girl, beaten, forced to walk the streets. This should not be happening in the United States of America.

As president, I directed my administration to step up our efforts—and we have. For the first time, at [Secretary of State Hillary Clinton's] direction, our annual trafficking report now includes the United States, because we can't ask other nations to do what we are not doing ourselves. We've expanded our interagency task force to include more federal partners, including the FBI [Federal Bureau of Investigation]. The intelligence community is devoting more resources to identifying trafficking networks. We've strengthened protections so that foreign-born workers know their rights.

And most of all, we're going after the traffickers. New anti-trafficking teams are dismantling their networks. Last year, we charged a record number of these predators with human trafficking. We're putting them where they belong—behind bars.

Barack Obama,
"Remarks by the President to the Clinton Global Initiative,"
WhiteHouse.gov, September 25, 2012.

Bringing in women from an outside source, as Martinez did, is just one of the ways human trafficking can manifest itself. The national survey of residential programs for victims of sex trafficking, conducted by the Illinois Criminal Justice Information Authority [ICJIA] and published in October 2013, examines the different forms and causes of sex trafficking.

Recruited into Slavery

Trafficking victims can often be recruited into the sex trade by someone they know, lured in by promises of money, drugs or attention. Victims may misinterpret the lifestyle as glamorous at first, before realizing they are unable to escape their situation.

Dan Emr, the executive director of Worthwhile Wear, an organization working to help victims of sex trafficking in Bucks and Montgomery Counties, added that women may enter the industry unknowingly.

"Sometimes, women will accept what they think is a legitimate job position, whether it's as a maid or something similar," he said. "By the time they realize the true nature of their work, it's too late for them to do anything about it—they are enslaved."

Victims can be recruited online, according to the ICJIA's 2013 report. Traffickers may use social media sites to initiate contact with victims and slowly gain their trust. Women are also recruited through misleading classified advertisements online.

Human trafficking is fluid, adaptable and under the radar. The secrecy and invisibility of the trafficking trade largely contributes to its success and growth.

Nationally, lawmakers are working to end the trade by giving it more attention and providing law enforcement with greater resources to prevent and halt the problem, Fitzpatrick said.

In a proclamation issued by President Barack Obama Dec. 30, he officially declared January 2014 to be National Slavery and Human Trafficking [Prevention] Month and outlined the necessity for addressing and ending this problem.

"Over a century and a half after President Abraham Lincoln issued the Emancipation Proclamation, millions remain in bondage—children forced to take part in armed conflict or sold to brothels by their destitute families, men and women who toil for little or no pay, who are threatened and beaten if they try to escape," reads the proclamation. "Slavery tears at our social fabric, fuels violence and organized crime, and debases our common humanity. During National Slavery and Human Trafficking Prevention Month, we renew our commitment to ending this scourge in all its forms."

VIEWPOINT 2

> *"Lie: 100,000–300,000 children are 'trafficked' every year in the United States."*

Sex Trafficking as a Worldwide Problem Is Exaggerated

Maggie McNeill

Maggie McNeill is an author, a media consultant, and a former sex worker. In the following viewpoint, she debunks a number of myths associated with prostitution and human trafficking. She argues, for example, that statistics that show that prostitutes die young, or that they are frequently raped or dissatisfied with their jobs, are inaccurate. She suggests that much of the panic surrounding prostitution and human trafficking is exaggerated and ends up putting women who work as prostitutes at risk.

As you read, consider the following questions:

1. What evidence does McNeill provide to show that the average prostitute does not enter the profession at age thirteen?

Maggie McNeill, "Frequently Told Lies," *The Honest Courtesan*, accessed June 5, 2015.

2. Where did the myth that human trafficking is the most profitable criminal enterprise originate, according to McNeill?

3. What does McNeill estimate is the true number of people enslaved in the world today?

Prohibitionists have a set of stock lies they can repeat in an article or Internet comment, so here is a reference to debunk them. . . .

Average Ages

LIE: The average age at which a woman enters prostitution is 13.

TRUTH: If this were true, there would have to be huge numbers of toddler-prostitutes to balance the many, many women who start later in life, such as to support themselves after divorce. Even underage prostitutes start at an average of 15–16, and only 15% of teen hookers (themselves a small minority of all sex workers) enter at an age below 13. A conservative estimate for the average age at which women enter the trade is 25. The "average debut at 13" lie was a purposeful distortion by anti-sex crusader Melissa Farley, who misrepresented the average age of first *noncommercial* sexual contact (which could include kissing, petting, etc.) reported by underage girls in one 1982 study as though it were the age they first reported selling sex; the actual average age at which the girls in that study began prostitution was 16.

LIE: The average age of death for a prostitute is 34.

TRUTH: That figure was derived from a 2003 study which examined all of the reports of murdered street workers in Colorado Springs from 1967–1999 and discovered that the average age of death of those victims was 34. In other words, nobody who *wasn't* murdered was included in the figure. It's like using the average age of dead soldiers in a war to proclaim "the average man who joins the military dies at 21."

LIE: The demonstrable problems with legalization schemes in places like Nevada and the Netherlands constitute an argument in favor of criminalization.

TRUTH: The demonstrable problems with those legalization schemes constitute an argument in favor of *de*criminalization. No sex worker rights organization in the world favors the Dutch or Nevada models, precisely because they *do* give rise to a host of problems which are prevented by treating sex work as work.

The Extent of Trafficking

LIE: 85% of prostitutes report childhood sexual abuse.

TRUTH: The original source for this claim was a 2004 study of incarcerated street workers which actually claimed that 45% reported sexual abuse and 85% physical abuse. Furthermore, there are serious methodological problems with the study, which is typical when biased researchers use an unrepresentative convenience sample and then extrapolate the results to a much larger population with which it does not correlate to any meaningful extent.

LIE: "End Demand" [laws criminalizing johns] tactics are an effective means of reducing prostitution.

TRUTH: Economic analysis demonstrates that "end demand" tactics increase the number of sales of sex, especially at the street level.

LIE: "Human trafficking" is the world's second most profitable criminal enterprise (or the third most, or most recently *the* most).

TRUTH: This myth originated in a UNODC [United Nations Office on Drugs and Crime] meeting where Kevin Bales (see "27 million" below) said, ". . . it's *impossible* to answer that question. If I *had to guess* I would say it was third. . . ." Ann Jordan surmised that the original source of the myth (later revealed as Bales) was probably thinking about *smuggling*, certainly a more credible candidate for the position.

LIE: Most of the violence to which sex workers are subjected is at the hands of clients or pimps.

TRUTH: Most of the violence suffered by sex workers in regimes where the work is fully or partially criminalized is at the hands of police.

LIE: Most or nearly all prostitutes are controlled by pimps and forced to work.

TRUTH: In nearly every stable modern society, the rate of coercion for adult prostitutes is about 2% or less, and for underage ones about 8–10%; this is roughly the same as the rate of non-sex-working women who report an abusive or controlling boyfriend or husband.

LIE: Most prostitutes are driven to it by financial need, and 9 out of 10 prostitutes would like to exit prostitution immediately.

TRUTH: These statements are probably true, but if there is any normal job (not an elite career occupied by a tiny fraction of the population) to which they do not apply, I'd like to know what it might be. What makes this a lie is the pretense that it applies to sex work to a higher degree than to other jobs, which it does not; one Australian study found that half of all prostitutes ranked their work as a "major source of satisfaction" in their lives, and 70% said they would definitely choose prostitution again if they had their lives to live over.

LIE: Most prostitutes are "recruited" into the work by pimps.

TRUTH: Most adult sex workers start due to pragmatic concerns, and most underage ones either think of it on their own or are recruited by friends.

LIE: Most prostitutes suffer symptoms of post-traumatic stress disorder [PTSD].

TRUTH: This is another of Melissa Farley's pet lies. She claims to be able to diagnose PTSD with a 15-minute self-administered questionnaire, despite the fact that the National Center for PTSD states that "*brief, single-item, closed-ended*

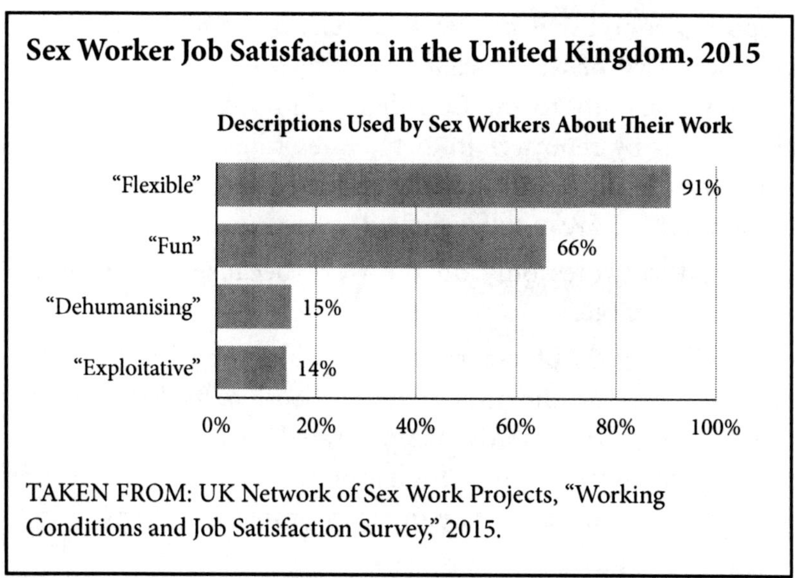

Sex Worker Job Satisfaction in the United Kingdom, 2015

TAKEN FROM: UK Network of Sex Work Projects, "Working Conditions and Job Satisfaction Survey," 2015.

questions for each PTSD symptom are . . . no more valid for making a diagnosis than self-report measures. . . . Proper assessment of PTSD is complex. . . ." In short, she is not qualified to diagnose this condition, and her method would be quackery even if she were.

LIE: Nearly all men buy sex *OR* a small, pathological group of men buys sex.

TRUTH: Though a slight majority of men have paid for sex at least once in their lives, about 20% of them do it "occasionally" (several times per year) and 6% "frequently."

Trafficked Children

LIE: 100,000–300,000 children are "trafficked" every year in the United States.

TRUTH: That myth is a distortion of an absurd estimate from the [Richard J.] Estes & [Neil Alan] Weiner study of 2001, which estimated that number of "children, adolescents and youth (up to 21) at risk of sexual exploitation." "Sex trafficking" was the *least* prevalent form of "exploitation" in their definition; other things they classed as "exploitation" included stripping, consensual homosexual relations and merely *viewing* porn. Two of the so-called "risk factors" were access to a car and proximity to the Canadian or Mexican border. When interviewed by reporters in 2011, Estes himself estimated the number of legal minors actually abducted into "sex slavery" as "*very small. . . . We're talking about a few hundred people.*"

LIE: Prostitutes only do the work because they have no meaningful choices.

TRUTH: 93% of escorts say they like their work for the money, 72% for the independence and 67% for meeting people. And a 2011 study demonstrated that most American escorts are women with "high opportunity cost," in other words those who have many other meaningful options.

LIE: Prostitutes spread disease.

TRUTH: Only about 3–5% of all STIs [sexually transmitted infections] can be attributed to either side of a sex work transaction, and the rates of infection among professionals are much (often dramatically) lower than among promiscuous amateurs.

Self-Esteem

LIE: Prostitution destroys the self-esteem of women involved in it.

TRUTH: Though only a small fraction of street workers report an increase in self-esteem after entering harlotry, they represent less than 15% of all prostitutes. 97% of escorts in one study reported an increase in self-esteem, compared with 50% of Nevada brothel workers; another study found that 75% of escorts felt their lives had improved since starting the work, 25% reported no change and 0% said their lives were worse. Anyone who has ever personally known any sex workers of any kind knows that if anything, their self-esteem is often *too* high.

LIE: Prostitution is associated with crime.

TRUTH: *Criminalization* is associated with crime. When "authorities" criminalize a consensual activity, they shouldn't be too surprised when criminals are then attracted to it. When's the last time you heard of anyone arrested for bootlegging or rum-running?

LIE: "Sex trafficking" increases when prostitution is legalized.

TRUTH: This claim is based on the deeply flawed [Eric] Neumayer, [Seo-Young] Cho and [Axel] Dreher study, which failed to even define the term "trafficking" in any way which would allow statistical comparison. The lie was further developed by a report in *Der Spiegel* which used figures for exploitation among *illegal* prostitutes to argue against legalization. In any legalization regime, those sex workers who are defined as being outside the legal structure (i.e., still criminal) are always those at greatest risk of violence and exploitation; to the extent that "trafficking" actually exists, it is generally the illegal nature of sex work which supplies the greatest tool for coercion. In the decriminalized structures of New Zealand and New South Wales, coercion is virtually nonexistent.

LIE: Sex work causes rape.

TRUTH: The evidence suggests that sex work of all kinds actually *decreases* the rates of rape, sexual assault, divorce and several other sex-related social ills.

LIE: The Swedish model [which criminalizes johns] has dramatically reduced prostitution and sex trafficking in Sweden.

TRUTH: The Swedish model cannot be shown to have had any effect on rates of prostitution *at all*, though it has made the lives of sex workers much more difficult and dangerous. Norwegian studies demonstrate that their version of the law has *increased* sex trafficking and the number of prostitutes, and also promoted pimping.

LIE: There are 27,000,000 people enslaved in the world today.

TRUTH: That number was developed by a “trafficking” fanatic named Kevin Bales using media reports multiplied by arbitrary numbers of his own devising; the more the hysteria, the higher the number of articles and thus the higher Bales’s number grows. “Trafficking” estimates are all over the map; the official UNODC estimate is less than a tenth as much (2.4 million), and even with vague, loose and ever-expanding definitions of “trafficking” the office has evidence for only about 40,000 in the entire world.

LIE: A very large fraction of sex workers are below 18.

TRUTH: In legal forms of sex work, virtually none are; in illegal forms the fraction is still very small. Only about 3.5% of prostitutes in Western countries are under 18.

VIEWPOINT 3

> *"So-called 'sex-trafficking' constitutes only a small percentage of all forced labor."*

Focusing on Sex Trafficking Distracts from Other Forms of Forced Labor

Melissa Gira Grant

Melissa Gira Grant is a writer and journalist as well as the author of Playing the Whore: The Work of Sex Work. *In the following viewpoint, she argues that trafficking is poorly defined. Many feminist and Christian anti-trafficking groups try to define trafficking as sexual exploitation of women, which can mean anything from sexual slavery to prostitution to appearing in pornography. She says that such a definition is problematic, however, because most forced labor and slavery are not sexual but instead involve agricultural work or other kinds of labor. Grant concludes that the current focus of trafficking discussions prevents a real focus on labor abuses.*

Melissa Gira Grant, "The Truth About Trafficking: It's Not Just About Sexual Exploitation," *Guardian*, October 24, 2012.

As you read, consider the following questions:

1. What groups does Grant list as part of the anti-trafficking coalition?
2. According to Grant, where does the White House get the statistic that one hundred thousand juveniles are victimized a year by trafficking?
3. How does the number of sex trafficking victims compare to the number of people in forced labor, according to International Labour Organization estimates?

Ending "trafficking" is perhaps the most well-known, well-resourced, well-loved social cause of the 21st century that doesn't require its proponents' agreement on what it even is they wish to end. What is "trafficking"? How many people are "trafficked"? Look beyond the surface of the fight against trafficking, and you will find misleading statistics and decades of debate over laws and protocols. As for the issue itself, the lack of agreement on how to define "trafficking" hasn't slowed campaigners' fight. Rather, defining trafficking has become their fight.

Defining Trafficking

Over the last 15 years, anti-trafficking campaigns have ascended to the most visible ranks of feminist, faith and human rights missions, enjoying support from organizations as ideologically unneighborly as women's rights NGO [nongovernmental organization] Equality Now and the conservative think tank the Heritage Foundation. The dominant contemporary understanding of trafficking took hold only around the turn of the century, driven in significant part by the advocacy of women's rights groups who sought to redefine trafficking specifically as the "sexual exploitation" of women and children. Indeed, this is the definition that groups like the Coalition Against Trafficking in Women succeeded in getting written into the first international laws related to trafficking. When many people hear about "trafficking," this is the picture that comes to mind, and it is one that women's rights groups—and, increasingly, evangelical Christian groups like Shared Hope International, International Justice Mission and Love146—use explicitly in their campaigning.

In fact, it is with the influence of these groups that the issue of trafficking itself began to migrate: from relative obscurity, to sessions at the United Nations, to highways in the United States, where drivers now find anti-trafficking billboards featuring shadowy photographs of young girls, images meant to "raise awareness." Using such images in service of ending "sexual exploitation" may seem contradictory, as the girls photographed are presented in what would otherwise seem to be a quasi-pornographic setting. A billboard I passed by last August on the interstate in Louisiana showed a girl who looked sweaty and wide-eyed—only with the words "NOT FOR SALE: END HUMAN TRAFFICKING" stamped in red over her face.

But what—and who—is being fought in what is pictured here?

Accurate statistics on trafficking are difficult to come by, which does not stop some anti-trafficking groups from using them anyway. For instance, Shared Hope International, which is aggressively pursuing anti-trafficking legislation in 41 US states, claims "at least 100,000 juveniles are victimized" each year in the United States, and possibly as many as 300,000—a figure that has been cited (repeatedly) by CNN. In truth, the figure is an estimate from a University of Pennsylvania report from 2001 of how many youth are "at-risk" of what its authors call "commercial sexual exploitation of a child," based on incidences of youth homelessness. But it was not a *count* of how many youth are victims of "trafficking," or involved in the sex trade.

Prostitution Conflated with Trafficking

Prostitution is often conflated with "trafficking" in these statistics, in part because the definition of trafficking that has been pushed to prominence refers exclusively to "sexual exploitation." In fact, this conflation has found its way into the collection of data. According to a report from the Global Alliance Against Trafficking in Women:

> "[W]hen statistics on trafficking are available, they usually refer to the number of migrant or domestic sex workers, rather than cases of trafficking."

This purposeful conflation of sex work and trafficking distinguishes the many feminist and faith-based anti-trafficking groups that focus on sex trafficking from groups that work directly with people who are involved in forced labor of all kinds, whether or not it involves sex work. This schism over who gets to define trafficking is about to come to a head for California voters in the form of Proposition 35, which, if passed this November [2012], will set higher criminal penalties and fines for those who commit what the authors of the bill define as sex-trafficking, as opposed to labor trafficking. It will also force those convicted of "trafficking" to register as sex offenders and submit to lifelong Internet monitoring—whether or not sex or the Internet were involved in their case. [Editor's note: Proposition 35 was passed in November 2012 with 81 percent of voters approving it.]

There is no question that California is home to several industries where, according to the Freedom Network (whose member organizations employ a human rights–based approach to anti-trafficking work), forced labor is known to occur: agricultural work, restaurant work, construction work, hotel work, garment work and sex work. But what unites the workers in these industries is not "commercial sexual exploitation," but the erosion of labor protections and the toughening up of immigration policies—which makes many more people vulnerable to coercion and abuse. Cindy Liou, staff attorney at the Asian Pacific Islander Legal Outreach, a Northern California–based project that has worked with hundreds of survivors of human trafficking, is advocating for Californians to vote no on this proposition.

> "It redefines trafficking in a way that's incorrect, confusing, and terrible. It's highly problematic because it does this at the expense of all trafficking victims—it ignores labor trafficking victims."

Not All Trafficking Is Sex Trafficking

In fact, so-called "sex-trafficking" constitutes only a small percentage of all forced labor, as estimated by the International Labour Organization [ILO]. In their 2012 report, the ILO categorizes "forced sexual exploitation" as distinct from other kinds of forced labor, which, in some ways, is helpful as not all forced labor involves sex, and in other ways, adds more confusion to the issue (because what distinguishes "sex-trafficking" from sexual abuse is its occurrence within a workplace or work relationship). Still, of the nearly 21 million people the ILO estimates are forced laborers, 4.5 million are estimated to be what the ILO calls "victims of forced sexual exploitation"—that is, over three-quarters of the people around the globe estimated to be in forced labor are *not* involved in "forced sexual exploitation." By contrast, the ILO estimates that 2.2 million people worldwide are forced laborers in prisons or in the military—people whose stories we are quite unlikely to find on a highway billboard.

But, as in the furor over "sex-trafficking," it would be wrong to let the volume of public outcry stand in for how significant a problem it is—however that issue is defined or ill-defined. Similarly, the push for "real numbers" can also lead us further into the ideological morass that itself defines the trafficking issue. Jo Doezema, a researcher with the Paulo

Longo Research Initiative and author of *Sex Slaves and Discourse Masters: The Construction of Trafficking*, cautions:

> "[E]ven a recognition that disputes over the meaning of trafficking involve politics and ideology does not go far enough: it still leaves intact the idea that trafficking can be defined satisfactorily, if political will, clear thinking, and practicality prevail."

That is, there can be no assessment of the severity of "trafficking" if we define this issue by a simple and coherent accounting of "victims." What's lost in the relentless defining and counting are the complex factors behind what is now almost unquestioningly called "trafficking." Most of all, what is lost is any understanding or appreciation of the challenges faced by the millions of people working, struggling and surviving in abusive conditions, whose experiences will never fit on a billboard.

Viewpoint 4

> *"In a lot of human trafficking cases there's no resolution because there's no cooperation, despite the fact that agreements are in place."*

Analysis: Southeast Asia's Human Trafficking Conundrum

IRIN

Integrated Regional Information Networks (IRIN) is a news agency focusing on humanitarian stories in regions that are underreported. In the following viewpoint, IRIN reports on the problem of human trafficking in Southeast Asia. The trafficking of women and underage girls for purposes of sexual exploitation is serious but difficult to quantify and prevent. The countries in the region are often reluctant to work with one another, making it difficult to coordinate anti-trafficking policies. In addition, local economies in poor regions sometimes center around trafficking and brothels, so local officials are unwilling to act.

IRIN, "Analysis: Southeast Asia's Human Trafficking Conundrum," irinnews.org, May 6, 2013.

As you read, consider the following questions:

1. According to IRIN, how does the 2000 UN protocol define human trafficking?
2. Which ASEAN governments have passed anti-trafficking legislation, according to IRIN?
3. Why does IRIN say that trafficking is becoming increasingly complex to prevent?

Tens of thousands of people are vulnerable to being trafficked in Southeast Asia, with governments struggling to understand and respond collectively to the problem, say experts and government officials.

A 2012 UN Office on Drugs and Crime (UNODC) report on human trafficking recorded more than 10,000 cases of trafficking in persons in South Asia, East Asia and the Pacific between 2007–2010, but it is unclear what the situation is today.

"Nobody has been able to convincingly demonstrate the scale of the problem, let alone come up with clear ways of how to address it," Sverre Molland, a lecturer at the Australian National University in Canberra who specializes in human trafficking, told IRIN.

"After all these years, we are still debating what trafficking actually is," he said, noting efforts to combat it were suffering from donor fatigue because of a lack of tangible results.

The 2000 UN Protocol to Prevent, Suppress and Punish Trafficking in Persons defines human trafficking as "the recruitment, transportation, transfer, harbouring or receipt of persons by means of coercion, abduction, fraud or deception, for the purpose of exploitation." Child trafficking is defined as the "recruitment, transportation, transfer, harbouring or receipt of a child for the purpose of exploitation."

In 2011, 16-year-old Evi* left her remote village in Indonesia's Banten province in the hope of making more money to help her family.

* not her real name

"My auntie introduced me to a broker who forged my travel documents so I could work," she said. "The broker then took me to a recruitment agency in Jakarta. I just wanted to earn more money. I thought God would protect me."

The agency arranged for Evi's travel to Jordan and placement as a domestic worker in Amman, but she soon found she was being exploited by her employer.

"I was allowed to sleep for about two hours a day, sometimes less," said Evi. "I had to take care of four children and clean the house. The mother and auntie of the children often beat me with sandals or punched me for no reason, and sometimes my nose bled."

In 2012, having endured physical abuse for over a year, her employer began to withhold her pay, and Evi attempted suicide by drinking a glass of kerosene.

"My employer found me unconscious and allowed me to rest, but the next day, they made me work again," she said.

Later, Evi ran away from her employer and roamed the streets of Amman looking for work until a local shopkeeper took her to a police station. Jordanian police then took her to the Indonesian embassy, which arranged for her repatriation to a shelter for trafficked children in Jakarta, where she is recovering.

Regional Cooperation

Cooperation between the 10 member states of the Association of Southeast Asian Nations (ASEAN) to tackle human trafficking has resulted in high-level initiatives and memorandums of understanding (MoUs).

"The MoUs should facilitate the exchanging of information and evidence between governments," said Sean Looney, operations, monitoring and evaluation manager at SISHA, an anti-trafficking and exploitation NGO in Phnom Penh, Cambodia.

"But in practice this does not happen at all. In a lot of human trafficking cases there's no resolution because there's no cooperation, despite the fact that agreements are in place."

According to Looney, cooperation was also hindered by a lack of trust between Cambodia and Thailand, and Cambodia and Vietnam, due in part to past conflicts.

Martin Reeve, a UNODC regional adviser on trafficking in Bangkok, said law enforcement agencies across the region were still developing.

"Securing a human trafficking conviction is at the best of times a difficult process," he said. "Intelligence-led policing is immature or non-existent, so the offenders arrested are less likely to be those organizing the trafficking, and police-to-police cooperation remains weak."

Many Cambodian men are trafficked annually.

All ASEAN governments are part of the Bali Process on People Smuggling, Trafficking in Persons and Related Transnational Crime, a non-binding, voluntary forum co-chaired by the governments of Indonesia and Australia, which began in 2002.

Febrian Ruddyard, director of international security and disarmament at the Indonesian Foreign Ministry, said the process had only recently begun to address trafficking in persons because not all countries had strong national legislation in place.

To date, all ASEAN governments have passed anti-trafficking legislation with the exception of Laos and Singapore.

Indonesia and Australia have faced challenges in encouraging members of the Bali Process to take practical action to address human trafficking, Ruddyard said.

"Many member countries are interested in the process but attracting funding from them [for projects] is difficult, not only because the issue is still a low priority in some countries but also because the process is non-binding," he said.

Ruddyard cited last year's creation of a regional support office in Bangkok to implement practical arrangements to combat trafficking, and a plan to use the Jakarta Centre for Law Enforcement Cooperation in Indonesia to train law enforcers across the region to better deal with human trafficking cases, as achievements of the process.

A Local Problem

Part of the problem lies at the local level.

Ahmad Sofian, national coordinator of ECPAT Indonesia, an NGO based in Jakarta working to end the commercial sexual exploitation of children, said there was little effort made by local law enforcement officials in Indonesia to deal with trafficking.

"There are economic benefits for those living close to the brothels that children are trafficked to," said Sofian. "Locals will gravitate to the area to sell food or provide security, and local police officers—often on low salaries—will ask for protection money from the owners of the brothels."

"This is why it's so difficult to eliminate trafficking," Sofian went on. "There's a local economy that grows up around it, and if the local government attempts to close these brothels, the police will become angry."

Jonhar Johan, an official at the Indonesian Women Empowerment and Child Protection Ministry, agreed, saying local implementation was a problem.

Poverty plays a deciding factor.

Of Indonesia's 497 districts, only 88 have anti-trafficking task forces.

"We need the commitment of district governments and police, but generally it is lacking," he said. "The districts need to develop their own task forces."

Johan also said that even when trafficking victims were identified and returned home by the authorities, they remained vulnerable to being re-trafficked.

The Difficulty of Defining Trafficking

Even when research on human trafficking has been undertaken, lack of conceptual clarity about the phenomenon has remained a significant obstacle. The international definition embodied in the UN [United Nations] Protocol to Prevent, Suppress and Punish Trafficking in Persons, Especially Women and Children, Supplementing the United Nations Convention Against Transnational Organized Crime (entry into force 2002)—commonly referred to as the Palermo protocols—does little to help:

> 'Trafficking in Persons' shall mean the recruitment, transportation, transfer, harbouring or receipt of persons, by the means of the threat or use of force or other forms of coercion, of abduction, of fraud, of deception, of the abuse of power or of a position of vulnerability, or of the giving or receiving of payments or benefits to achieve the consent of a person having control over another person, for the purposes of exploitation. Exploitation shall include, at a minimum, the exploitation of the prostitution of others or other forms of sexual exploitation, forced labour or services, slavery or practices similar to slavery, servitude or the removal of organs.

This extremely convoluted definition was the result of fierce wrangling and ideological debate, the outcome of which satisfied few involved in its formulation and resulted in much mutual recrimination.

David A. Feingold, "Trafficking, Trade and Migration: Mapping Human Trafficking in the Mekong Region," An Atlas of Trafficking in Southeast Asia: The Illegal Trade in Arms, Drugs, People, Counterfeit Goods and Resources. *Ed. Pierre-Arnaud Chouvy. New York: I.B. Tauris, 2013.*

"We offer them financial help so they can start up small businesses when they return home, but when we visit them to formalize this, we find they've gone," he said. "Many victims are poor and they see the economic gain from working abroad, so maybe they leave home again because of the money. Traffickers like these kinds of people."

According to SISHA's Looney, while the Cambodian police's anti–human trafficking and juvenile protection division tackled human trafficking, at the district level police were hamstrung by a lack of funds.

"The police have to use their own money for fuel to go to interview victims, bring victims to court and feed the victims [while they are in police custody]," he said. "They don't have access to basic operational costs, and it's unclear whether that's down to ineptitude, a lack of funds, or whether funds are being siphoned off elsewhere."

SISHA was financially supporting police investigations into human trafficking and offering guidance on conducting criminal investigations, said Looney.

"Many local police officers are just looking for support so they can do their jobs. The average police officer wants to tackle the problem and help victims, but practical requirements make it difficult for them," he said.

Increasing Complexity

International Organization for Migration (IOM) Indonesia chief of mission Denis Nihill said the changing nature of human trafficking made it more difficult to tackle.

"There's been a lot of work done on the Greater Mekong Region for many years on trafficking, but it's become more complex, as it's now inextricably woven with labour migration, which is a much more difficult nut to crack because it is less easy to detect than trafficking linked to the sex industry."

Nihill also pointed to the difficulties of tackling internal trafficking, which IOM's 2011 counter-trafficking report highlighted as particularly problematic in Indonesia.

"For cross-border trafficking, people must pass through the hands of several government agencies, but internally trafficked people need not come to the attention of any officials, so in many ways it's a more alarming situation," he said.

The US Department of State's 2012 Trafficking in Persons Report categorizes most ASEAN countries as Tier 2, meaning they do not fully comply with minimum standards for the elimination of trafficking, but are making significant efforts to do so.

Viewpoint 5

> "At the very least, the Mam scandal should make prostitution 'abolitionists' think hard about their allies, their facts and their tactics."

Opportunists Profit from Panic over Sex Trafficking in Southeast Asia

Katha Pollitt

Katha Pollitt is a columnist for the Nation *and the author of* Subject to Debate: Sense and Dissents on Women, Politics, and Culture. *In the following viewpoint, she reports that Somaly Mam, a leading anti-trafficking advocate in Cambodia, has been embroiled in a scandal. Reporters have uncovered evidence that Mam lied about her own life story as a trafficking victim and that she encouraged others to lie as well. Pollitt says that the falsehoods raise difficult questions for anti-trafficking groups, which may have overstated the extent of trafficking in Cambodia and may support policies such as brothel raids that put women at risk of police violence. Pollitt suggests reassessing anti-trafficking policies given the Mam revelations.*

Katha Pollitt, "Sex Trafficking, Lies & Money: Lessons from the Somaly Mam Scandal," Thenation.com, June 23–30, 2014.

As you read, consider the following questions:

1. According to the viewpoint, who is Greg Mortenson, and how is his story similar to Somaly Mam's?
2. Why does Pollitt argue that Kristof should have known about problems with Mam's story earlier?
3. According to Melissa Gira Grant, how did Mam's actions harm sex workers in Cambodia?

First Greg Mortenson, the world-famous author of *Three Cups of Tea*, raised millions of dollars for schools in Afghanistan and Pakistan that turned out not to exist. Now Somaly Mam, the world-famous Cambodian campaigner against sex trafficking, one of *Time*'s 100 Most Influential People in the World, has stepped down from her eponymous foundation in the wake of charges that she fabricated her harrowing autobiography of having been sold into sex slavery as a child. According to an exposé in *Newsweek*, Mam had a normal childhood and adolescence and is remembered by neighbors as "a happy, pretty girl with pigtails." Not only did Mam apparently invent her past, she allegedly coached others in her organization, AFESIP, to tell similarly lurid false tales. Long Pross, who has just stepped down as a spokeswoman for the Somaly Mam Foundation, claimed a pimp gouged out her eye; actually, her eye was removed in surgery for a tumor when she was 13. She was never in a brothel. Meas Rotha says Mam auditioned girls for public appearances and told her she had to lie to help other women.

Somaly Mam

I hope by the time you read these words, Nicholas Kristof will have written more about this than the short blog post available as we go to press, in which he said he is withholding judgment and promised to "poke around" more. Kristof heavily promoted Mam in his *New York Times* column as "one of my heroes," accompanied her on "rescues" of girls being held in brothels and pretty much swallowed whole everything she told him—for example, that her 14-year-old daughter had been kidnapped and raped by traffickers in revenge for Mam's work (according to Mam's ex-husband, the girl ran off with a boyfriend). Until the other day, she was featured on the PBS website for his documentary *Half the Sky*, in which she appeared. I'm not holding my breath, though: Kristof promoted Mortenson, too, and when the bad news came down, chalked his malfeasance up to "disorganization."

What is the old adage? Fool me once...

I will gladly grant that it isn't easy to figure out what really goes on in NGOs [nongovernmental organizations] far away, or even near at hand. Every year I worry that a group I feature in my holiday donations column will turn out to be less than meets the eye. But Kristof was not, like me, sitting at a desk in Manhattan. He is a world-traveling, Pulitzer Prize–winning journalist who spent plenty of time in Cambodia and had all the resources of the *Times* at his command. Moreover, suspicion about Mam had been building for some time. The English-language *Cambodia Daily* has been publishing investigative reports on her for the past two years. Is it asking too much of a newspaperman that he should read the papers?

There are many lessons to be learned from this debacle. Here's one: When people tell you what you want to hear, watch out. Americans love stories about heroic individuals—victims who surmount horror through grit and pluck, and ordinary people who change the world because of one simple idea. It helps if the heroic individual speaks English, is telegenic and charismatic, and can mingle comfortably with international celebrities and CEOs [chief executive officers]. The structure of big money philanthropy—gala benefits and fancy awards ceremonies and PBS documentaries and access to major journalists like Kristof—favors such people. Mam had support from the State Department and from A-listers like Ange-

The Danger of Trafficking Crackdowns

Measures taken in the name of preventing or otherwise addressing trafficking and related exploitation often have a highly adverse impact on individual rights and freedoms that are protected under international law. Evidence-based examples of such "negative human rights externalities" include many of the practices identified in this book such as: detention of trafficked persons in immigration or shelter facilities; prosecution of trafficked persons for status-related offenses including illegal entry, illegal stay, and illegal work; denial of exit or entry visas or permits; entry bans; compulsory medical examinations; raids, rescues, and "crackdowns" that do not include full consideration of and protection for the rights of individuals involved; forced repatriation of victims in danger of reprisals or re-trafficking; conditional provision of support and assistance; denial of a right to a remedy; and violations of the rights of persons suspected or convicted of involvement in trafficking and related offenses, including unfair trials and inappropriate sentencing. These practices, still commonplace in many countries, underscore the strong relationship between trafficking and human rights, as well as the fundamental importance of the international guardians of the relevant instruments, including the human rights treaty bodies, using the full range of tools at their disposal to hold states accountable for their actions and omissions.

Anne T. Gallagher,
The International Law of Human Trafficking.
New York: Cambridge University Press, 2010.

lina Jolie, Susan Sarandon, Sheryl Sandberg and Queen Sofia of Spain. The competition for attention and money fuels exaggerations and distortions and fabrications—both of the problem and its solutions.

A Challenge to Abolitionists

What does this scandal say about the degree of coercion involved in sex work, a subject of much debate among feminists? Did Mam use fake trafficking victims in her promotional campaigns because they were better than real ones at conveying a Western image of what a trafficking victim looks like? On the *Times* op-ed page, Melissa Gira Grant argued persuasively that Mam not only hugely inflated the amount of sex slavery in Cambodia, but that she harmed the very people she claimed to help by using the police to harass and detain those "rescued" in her brothel raids and by threatening the girls and women who tried to leave her programs.

At the very least, the Mam scandal should make prostitution "abolitionists" think hard about their allies, their facts and their tactics. So far, I haven't seen many signs of that. "She was so passionate about her work," Jessica Neuwirth, founder of Equality Now, told me, sounding sad and bewildered, "so full of conviction about what she was doing." Although Neuwirth says Equality Now never gave Mam money, it was a major promoter of her work. Mam's autobiography, *The Road of Lost Innocence*, gets a page to itself on their website. But, Neuwirth went on, "people aren't saying she pocketed the funds. I haven't heard anyone say her work isn't impressive." And most important, "this doesn't change anything about the situation in Cambodia. We have no doubt these things happen on a large scale." The goal remains the same: to shut down the brothels.

New Tactics Needed

I've never supported brothel raids, which are potentially violent and wide open to the exact sort of coercion and corruption abolitionists attribute to the brothels themselves. It's not as if the Cambodian police force is Jane Addams [an early 20th-century social worker] at Hull House. At the same time, I'm less comforted than Gira Grant by the statistics she cites: that 88 percent of Cambodian sex workers are not coerced and that 76 percent of supposed trafficking victims "had a prior knowledge that they would engage in prostitution-related activities." Leaving aside all the problems with collecting reliable data in this extralegal area (and other studies show different figures), one in eight and one in four are a lot of people.

That the most horrifying stories promoted by Mam are rare or outright lies is good news. But the teenager stuck in sex work because of poverty is real. Wouldn't it make sense now for Mam's supporters to focus on that girl's complex reality?

VIEWPOINT 

"Any time you have a large number of people gathering in one place, especially males, and it's a party atmosphere, it's prime ground for sex trafficking."

Sex Trafficking Spikes at the Super Bowl

Lane Anderson

Lane Anderson is a writer for the Deseret News. *In the following viewpoint, she writes that sex trafficking increases at sporting events such as the Super Bowl. She reports on researchers from Arizona State University who measured a spike in online ads for sexual services around the time of the Super Bowl. Many of the ads, the researchers say, involve trafficked or kidnapped women and girls. Anderson says that increased awareness around Super Bowl sex trafficking and increased law enforcement efforts may decrease the amount of trafficking.*

As you read, consider the following questions:

1. What evidence does Anderson provide that trafficking was a problem during the Super Bowls of 2010 and 2011?

Lane Anderson, "The Super Bowl Is the Largest Human Trafficking Event in the Country," *Deseret News*, January 30, 2015.

2. How does sex trafficking at the Super Bowl compare to trafficking at other sporting events, according to the viewpoint?
3. What baffles Dominique Roe-Sepowitz about responses to online ads for sexual services?

Last February [2014], Texas attorney general Greg Abbott declared the Super Bowl the "single largest human trafficking incident in the U.S."

Now, Arizona activists are looking to prevent trafficking for the sporting event this weekend.

Over 10,000 "prostitutes"—many of whom were trafficking victims—were brought into Miami for the Super Bowl in 2010, and during the Dallas Super Bowl in 2011, there were 133 arrests for sex with minors, according to the National Center for Missing and Exploited Children.

The enormity of the sporting event provides an ideal setting for traffickers to cash in, says Nita Belles, anti-trafficking activist and author of *In Our Backyard*, an account of trafficking in the U.S.

"Any time you have a large number of people gathering in one place, especially males, and it's a party atmosphere, it's prime ground for sex trafficking," says Belles.

Dubious History

Researchers from Arizona State University [ASU] studied online sex ads for 10 days surrounding last year's Super Bowl in New Jersey, and found that ad volume spiked leading up to the event, and dissipated afterward. At least half appeared to involve sex trafficking victims.

Dominique Roe-Sepowitz, lead author and professor of social work at ASU, is repeating similar research in Arizona for comparison. She's only a few days into monitoring in Arizona, but already the numbers are upsetting, she says.

"The sheer number of ads would be beyond what any one law enforcement agency could respond to," said Sepowitz, who said that there are thousands of ads and responses to those ads.

The week before the Super Bowl in Indianapolis in 2012, over 1,000 postings on Backpage.com—an online postings site with space for "adult entertainment" services—listed services from women and escort services, and a quarter referenced the Super Bowl, or "Super Bowl Specials," according to a *Forbes* report.

What's still unclear is how much sex trafficking the Super Bowl attracts compared to other events like a Jets game or Giants game, says Sepowitz. Further data are needed to determine that.

Traffickers work the activities surrounding the game, says Belles, at parties and popular bars.

"There are Playboy parties in town, a [rapper] Snoop Dogg party," says Belles, who is in Phoenix to do awareness work during the game weekend. That's where traffickers will be working the crowd to find customers. They also use the Internet.

Last year, the day before the Super Bowl, over 100 arrests were made in Manhattan based on Backpage.com ads and the crackdown received a lot of media attention. Sepowitz believes that the increased attention and law enforcement could lead to a decrease in criminal behavior surrounding the Super Bowl.

"I think if you are a trafficker and a pimp, and you bring a person here to be trafficked, you are asleep at the wheel," she said, especially in Arizona where law enforcement started doing busts months ago to discourage sex buyers.

"There are lots of men and lots of money here, and that's what any market needs for sexual exploitation," she said, but the NFL [National Football League], law enforcement and community have "sent a message."

The Problem Is Demand

The major findings of the report are that trafficking is a national problem—not just during the Super Bowl, says Sepowitz.

"Like every other city in this country, trafficking happens here every day," she said.

The problem is driven by demand, which creates an extremely lucrative business. The only way to address that, Sepowitz says, is by sending the message that purchasing people for sex is illegal and harshly punished.

"We're concerned about young men and boys getting the message that buying and selling human beings is okay," she said. "We can change that."

Part of Sepowitz's job is to place decoy ads and get the responses. She's always baffled that the men respond with details about themselves, how they look, what they do. There's a delusion that these women are working for themselves and enjoy their work, she says. "All those women care about is that they meet their quota and get the money to their pimp or trafficker," she says. Otherwise, they often face dire consequences. Ads perpetuate this myth, often worded as though they are written by the women themselves, and that they "can't wait" to meet their buyers.

Belles notes that law enforcement and language have been changing, and need to change, to shift responsibility. "Prostitutes" are usually victims, she says, and "john" is too nice a word for someone who should be called a "sex buyer."

Sepowitz is heartened by changes in law enforcement that have started to focus on treatment for women arrested in the sex trade, rather than prosecution.

"There's a saying that prostitution is the oldest profession in the world," says Belles. "But it's the oldest abuse in the world."

Viewpoint 7

"The persistence of the Super Bowl sex trafficking myth can be credited to the theatrical quality of its anecdotes."

Sex Trafficking Does Not Spike at the Super Bowl

Susan Elizabeth Shepard

Susan Elizabeth Shepard is a writer in Austin. In the following viewpoint, she argues that sex trafficking does not spike at the time of the Super Bowl. She says there is no evidence of increased arrests for trafficking or incidents of trafficking during the yearly event, and the myths surrounding these issues have been debunked over and over again. The myths persist, however, which distracts from real issues regarding trafficking such as forced labor for the construction of World Cup buildings in Qatar. She concludes that myths surrounding trafficking at the Super Bowl lead to confused and uninformed public policy.

As you read, consider the following questions:

1. According to the viewpoint, how many arrests for trafficking around the time of the Super Bowl were there in 2011, 2012, and 2013?

Susan Elizabeth Shepard, "The Sex Trafficking Super Bowl Myth," sportsonearth.com, January 29, 2014.

2. What does "Diana" say about her experiences as an escort at Super Bowl time?
3. Before the myths of sex trafficking, what other myths about gendered violence were linked to the Super Bowl, according to Shepard?

In 2011, Texas attorney general Greg Abbott said that the Super Bowl is "commonly known as the single largest human trafficking incident in the United States." Ever since that moment, dozens of stories have appeared about the sex trafficking at the Super Bowl, and this year [2014] is no different. For three years running, NFL [National Football League] spokesperson Brian McCarthy has been telling reporters that the Super Bowl's status as a human trafficking nexus is an urban legend. Abbott's office has not responded to inquiries about the information or sources on which he based his comments.

Urban Legend

In November, Cindy McCain said the NFL is lagging behind in taking a stand on human trafficking, and she joined Sen. Amy Klobuchar (D-Minn.) to discuss the subject with league officials in January. "Many NGOs [nongovernmental organizations] that work this issue on a day-to-day basis that are on the streets say, and I believe it because I've seen it, that the Super Bowl is the largest human trafficking venue," McCain said. Unfortunately, she said it at the very end of an interview, and she's never explained what *exactly* it was that she had seen. Perhaps she saw the trafficking documentary *Tricked*, whose central subject, sex trafficking survivor Danielle Douglas, told the AP [Associated Press]: "They're coming to the Super Bowl not even to watch football. They're coming to the Super Bowl to have sex with women and/or men or children."

The NFL has a history of denying or minimizing nascent scandals, so perhaps McCarthy's denials carry minimal weight. In this case, however, the league's spokesman is right. Reporters and anti-trafficking organizations have been refuting the claim that the Super Bowl attracts sex trafficking for years. In 2011, when Abbott made his statement, there were "zero arrests for trafficking in the time frame surrounding the Super Bowl," says public information officer Sherri Jeffrey with the Dallas Police Department. The next year, in Indianapolis? Two. Last year, in New Orleans? Two. Even those charges weren't brought against criminal masterminds, running global rings of child prostitution; they were against garden-variety pimps. Criminals, yes, but participants in "the single largest human trafficking incident"? No. Far from it.

Yet this sensational narrative—crime, sex, money and The Big Game—persists. January is now National Slavery and Human Trafficking Prevention Month, and as this year's game in New Jersey approaches, public officials and volunteers are compelled to take Super Bowl–related action, regardless of the reality. The stories keep coming, most recently from Laura Dimon at PolicyMic (which ran a similar story last year), faithfully repeating claims so outlandish . . . that a *Dallas Morning News* reporter felt compelled to join in the reader comments to say so. Just one day later, PolicyMic updated the story with an editor's note, noting that corrections had been made.

Prostitution Classified as Trafficking

One might wonder, in light of all this coverage, just how interested football fans, corporate sponsors and the media corps are in paying for sex with trafficked people.

Any actual nexus for human trafficking would require a larger-than-normal number of willing buyers. Sports fans would need to be willing to risk arrest away from home, in addition to desiring commercial sex from coerced victims, possibly underage ones. The Global Alliance Against Traffic in Women wrote in a 2011 report: "This simplistic equation relies on problematic assumptions about masculinity, business practices within the sex industry, sex workers' capacity to take action, and the root causes of trafficking." After reviewing reports from the [FIFA] World Cup, the Olympics and the Super Bowl, the report concluded that there was no evidence of increased human trafficking at sporting events. "There's not an enormous amount of data that tells the story that there's a giant spike in trafficking around the Super Bowl," said Polaris Project CEO [chief executive officer] Bradley Myles in an interview with *USA Today*.

Traffickers also would have to see a profitable opportunity where independent sex workers apparently do not. "Diana," an independent escort who frequently travels with clients, said the Super Bowl is one event she's never been invited to, professionally. "I've attended other, smaller-scale games with clients, but I've never been invited to the Super Bowl. Those who've gone take male friends or male family members," she said. "And I've never once heard of an escort planning a tour around working the Super Bowl, not even those women who tour regularly." To track if men were more likely to buy sex at sporting events, anthropologist Dr. Laura Agustin says researchers would have to shadow fans. "I'd have to be sure to be on the same plane with them, and then get there and hang out and see how much drink they've had, and how they feel when they watch football, and how many of them go to pay for sex. You can't do this research!"

One piece of evidence held up to prove an increase in Super Bowl–related trafficking is the count of Backpage[.com] ads—but in order to give significance to that count, one must assume that the increase comes from sex traffickers, rather than independent sex workers seeking to capitalize on tourist traffic. Nobody would mistake an increase in postings for domestic, construction and agricultural workers for evidence of a major nexus of forced labor. Despite this, law enforcement and journalists often classify all prostitution as trafficking, making it even harder to find reliable numbers.

Regardless of whether someone is engaged in sex work willingly or through coercion, it is still a criminal act in almost all parts of the country. As a result, efforts like those that precede the Super Bowl do little to aid victims, according to Elizabeth Ricks, an attorney who works with the Transformative Justice Law Project of Illinois. "With everything illegal, it becomes this gray area, and what I'm seeing in my work is that the trafficking victims are really getting lost in the conversation," she said. "If we had decriminalization, the difference between consensual sex work and trafficking would be much more stark." When the type of labor is legal, like domestic or agricultural work, there is less discretion required of law enforcement to determine if someone is a victim unlike in cases of suspected sex trafficking. "It's the difference between sex and rape," Ricks said. "It would really become very clear that consensual sex work is not the same as having to perform labor under coercion or threat."

The use of "human trafficking" to refer exclusively to sex trafficking is yet another concern for advocates of trafficking victims. Forced domestic and manual labor are much larger problems, according to the International Labour Organization, and the Global Alliance Against Traffic in Women points out that sporting events may draw other forms of trafficking—for example, the trafficking of workers to construct the playing grounds and lodging for events like the Olympics and the World Cup. Qatar's *kafala* system [in which migrant workers cannot change jobs] has been a focal point for human rights groups concerned about worker abuses during World Cup construction, and Human Rights Watch has documented abuses of workers during preparations for the Sochi [Russia] Olympics. If there is an increase in human trafficking connected to sporting events, there is more evidence that it happens long before fans arrive, rather than catering to them.

Melodramatic Rhetoric

The persistence of the Super Bowl sex trafficking myth can be credited to the theatrical quality of its anecdotes. McCain's activism originated with an experience she had while shopping in Calcutta. She heard noises under the shop floor and looked down. "I could see all these little eyes looking up at me, and I realized it was probably 30 little girls, looking up through the floorboards at me," she said. "I realized at that time that it was very serious, and these girls were either enslaved or being trafficked, but the kicker was [that] I walked out of that shop, and I never did anything." Afterward, McCain approached Arizona governor Jan Brewer to propose taking action on trafficking, and the state's Task Force on Human Trafficking was created.

Agustin notes that many descriptions of trafficking in the U.S. employ a similar, lurid tone. "Incredible language is used, like 'the dark underbelly' and 'the forbidden fruit,' 'lost childhoods.' It's all melodramatic rhetoric from the 19th century," she said.

Alaskan activist Tara Burns agrees. "The public is honestly misinformed. They see these sex-trafficking [public service] advertisements, with pictures of innocent little white girls in pigtails being kidnapped by evil men, and they believe that's what's happening. The reality is that most people who are sex trafficked are already marginalized by society—runaways, homeless people and sex workers—and most sex trafficking looks a lot like domestic violence or exploitative or abusive labor practices."

To be clear, this is not to say that the victims of sex trafficking aren't sympathetic or deserving of the full support of law enforcement, but manipulating the images of such practices only serves to perpetuate a fiction when the reality is stark enough. Even Douglas, the trafficking survivor, has written about the way media tries to control or alter her story to fit preconceived notions and why that can be dangerous.

NFL Domestic Violence and Sex Trafficking Myths

Urban myths were the original viral content. Combine one with modern communications, and they can have as many re-

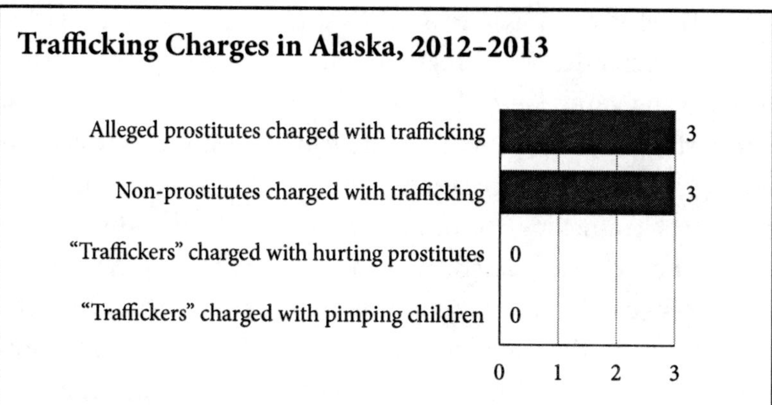

TAKEN FROM: Tara Burns, "People in Alaska's Sex Trade: Their Lived Experiences and Policy Recommendations," 2014.

buttals as confirmations, yet still retain a grip on public imagination. The sex trafficking myth is only the most recent "single largest" Super Bowl narrative. For over 20 years, the Super Bowl also has been cited as the day with the single largest number of domestic violence incidents. This too is a myth, and its genesis illustrates how using a large event to raise consciousness about an issue can result in confusion and false association. It started with a public service announcement [PSA], which aired during the 1993 Super Bowl. In a subsequent *New York Times* op-ed ("Violence Translates at Home"), Robert Lipsyte drew a line connecting viewers of on-field violence with spousal abuse. Ever since, the correlation has been both decried by activists and used to dismiss them. Every year, there are stories that debunk the domestic violence myth. Activists say it actually hurts their cause to have inaccurate information out there.

Political hay is made easily from myths, driving state legislatures and interest groups to respond with new laws, even for good causes. That 1993 PSA helped marshal support for the Violence Against Women Act. In the trafficking task force reports of Texas, Indiana and Arizona, though, the impending

Super Bowl is cited as a reason for implementing ever stricter laws and penalties for things that are already crimes. (It isn't as if forcing someone to have sex for money, or moving them across state lines to do so, had any legal loopholes that needed closing.) That new legislation rarely if ever actually protects victims of trafficking, according to Burns. "In the almost two years since it was passed, Alaska's sex trafficking laws have only been used against people who were also charged with prostitution in the same case, and never against someone who wasn't accused of being a sex worker themselves," she said.

These myths about women suffering on Super Bowl Sunday can feel true, because there is sufficient negative coverage about the NFL and violence against women. The NFL has had real domestic violence issues, involving the actions of players and the league's inconsistent response to those actions. Some players get cut, while others experience no professional or league censure. In the last five years, there have been exactly as many Super Bowl appearances by players accused of sexual assault as trafficking arrests in Super Bowl host cities—six of each—yet far more resources have been devoted to ferreting out the latter.

In 2011, Erin Gloria Ryan wrote about the difficulty of enjoying a Super Bowl with a league where sexual assault seems routine, especially when Ben Roethlisberger [football player twice accused of sexual assault] is at the head of a team. Ryan's concerns accurately reflect at least part of the league's image issues. It would be an oversimplification to say, "People wouldn't so easily believe football fans were out there paying for sex slaves if they weren't cheering accused rapists so enthusiastically." At the same time, for many who have been victims of domestic violence or systematic sexual assault for profit, a league in which people accused and convicted of sexual assault seem to escape harsh penalties, does not appear to be an ally.

Sexual violence allegations are certainly part of the league's recent past, and a myth about domestic violence has been part of Super Bowl Sunday's for 20 years. That image makes the concept of the Super Bowl as a massive sex trafficking event just believable enough—regardless of the truth.

Periodical and Internet Sources Bibliography

The following articles have been selected to supplement the diverse views presented in this chapter.

Bruce Alpert	"Human Trafficking Draws Attention During Super Bowl, but It's a Year-Long, Worldwide Problem," *Times-Picayune* (New Orleans, LA), January 30, 2015.
Elizabeth Nolan Brown	"Did You Hear About the Sex Traffickers Abducting Grown Women from Hobby Lobby?," Reason.com, June 8, 2015.
Lisa Curtis and Olivia Enos	"Combating Human Trafficking in Asia Requires U.S. Leadership," Heritage Foundation, February 26, 2015.
Elise Hilton	"Is Asia Getting Out of the Human Trafficking Business?," Acton Institute, June 8, 2015.
Glenn Kessler	"The False Claim That Human Trafficking Is a '$9.5 Billion Business' in the United States," *Washington Post*, June 2, 2015.
Annette Lyth	"Why Southeast Asia Struggles to Tackle Modern-Day Slavery," Deutsche Welle, September 4, 2015.
Charles Parkinson	"Southeast Asia Has a Plan to Tackle Human Trafficking, but There's an Elephant in the Room," Vice News, May 18, 2015.
James Queally	"National Sex Trafficking Sting Nets Nearly 600 Arrests Before Super Bowl," *Los Angeles Times*, February 2, 2015.
Straits Times (Asia)	"5 Things to Know About Human Trafficking in South-East Asia," May 12, 2015.

Chapter 3

How Does Legal Policy Toward Sex Work Affect Sex Trafficking?

Chapter Preface

Many politicians and activists argue that advertising venues that allow advertising of sexual services can create markets for sex trafficking. Much recent attention has focused on Backpage.com, a classified ad website that was associated with the *Village Voice* but has been sold to undisclosed owners.

Anti-trafficking organizations argue that traffickers advertise the services of trafficked women and children through the site, enabling exploitation and violence. "Backpage.com has consciously chosen, as a business, to continue to profit from modern-day slavery," Penny Venetis, director of Rutgers International Human Rights Clinic, wrote after Backpage.com refused to close its adult services section, as reported by NJ.com.

Tod Robberson of the *Dallas Morning News* offered more details about how Backpage.com provides information about adult services. Robberson reports he found a site called Eccieleaks, which has explicit discussions about escorts and prostitutes and the services they provide. "It works like this: Backpage.com posts an ad for a 'massage' parlor somewhere in Dallas. Participants go to Eccieleaks, provide an informational link to Backpage, then describe what happens at the massage parlor or strip club or hotel or wherever the service is provided." Robberson says that Backpage.com is not responsible for the content of Eccieleaks, but he argues that Backpage nonetheless profits from the discussions on Eccieleaks and from the sale of adult services. He suggests that this ultimately promotes trafficking.

Other writers, however, argue that Backpage.com does not promote trafficking and that it actually reduces violence in the sex industry. One woman named Maria, who sells sexual services to supplement her income as a hairdresser and an artist, said in an article for the Daily Beast, that Backpage.com is a safe way for her to work. "If Backpage and the many other adult services sites were to be removed as an option for [men and women like me]," she said, "I fear we will be forced to the streets, where the most abuse occurs." Another woman, a single mother named Zoe, said in the same article that if Backpage .com were shut down, she would be at risk of being homeless. "I've never been a streetwalker, but to have to go to that as an option puts me at much greater risk of harm than having the control over who my clients are when I post on such sites."

Alison Bass writing at the *Huffington Post* argues that shutting down Backpage.com not only hurts the women who advertise on the site but also does little to curb trafficking. "Media reports about the controversy over Backpage often neglect to mention that shutting down such online classified sites does not curb trafficking. Indeed, police who investigate trafficking cases say it merely pushes the practice further underground and makes it more difficult for them to investigate the trafficking of underage prostitutes or illegal migrants," she points out. Backpage.com became a center of adult services listings after Craigslist shut down its erotic services site. It seems likely that if Backpage was closed, another site would simply open to take its place.

The following chapter looks at other controversies surrounding legal restrictions on adult services and the effects such restrictions may or may not have on reducing trafficking.

VIEWPOINT 1

"On average, countries with legalized prostitution experience a larger degree of reported human trafficking inflows."

Legalizing Sex Work Increases Sex Trafficking

Seo-Young Cho, Axel Dreher, and Eric Neumayer

Seo-Young Cho is a professor at the German Institute for Economic Research; Axel Dreher is a professor at Heidelberg University; and Eric Neumayer is a professor at the London School of Economics and Political Science. In the following viewpoint, they argue that in theory, legalizing prostitution will create a greater demand for sexual services. It is unclear whether this will increase trafficking (because of increased demand) or reduce trafficking (because it is easier and less risky to buy legal sexual services). The authors' research suggests that overall trafficking increases when prostitution is legalized. They emphasize, however, that legalizing prostitution may have other benefits.

As you read, consider the following questions:

1. Why do the authors believe that legalizing prostitution will not reduce trafficking to zero?

Reprinted from World Development, 41(1), Seo-Young Cho, Axel Dreher, and Eric Neumayer, "Does Legalized Prostitution Increase Human Trafficking?," pp. 67–82, Copyright (2013), with permission from Elsevier.

2. According to the viewpoint, what are prostitution laws like in Sweden, Denmark, and Germany?
3. What do the authors suggest might be some benefits of legalizing prostitution?

Much recent scholarly attention has focused on the effect of globalization on human rights and women's rights in particular. Yet, one important, and largely neglected, aspect of globalization with direct human rights implications is the increased trafficking of human beings, one of the dark sides of globalization. Similarly, globalization scholars with their emphasis on the apparent loss of national sovereignty often neglect the impact that domestic policies crafted at the country level can still exert on aspects of globalization. This [viewpoint] analyzes how one important domestic policy choice—the legal status of prostitution—affects the incidence of human trafficking inflows to countries.

Prostitution and Trafficking

Most victims of international human trafficking are women and girls. The vast majority end up being sexually exploited through prostitution. Many authors therefore believe that trafficking is caused by prostitution and combating prostitution with the force of the law would reduce trafficking. For example, [D.] Hughes maintains that "evidence seems to show that legalized sex industries actually result in increased trafficking to meet the demand for women to be used in the legal sex industries." [M.] Farley suggests that "wherever prostitution is legalized, trafficking to sex industry marketplaces in that region increases." In its "Trafficking in Persons Report," the U.S. State Department states as the official U.S. government position "that prostitution is inherently harmful and dehumanizing and fuels trafficking in persons." The idea that combating human trafficking requires combating prostitution is, in fact, anything but new. As [J.] Outshoorn points out, the

UN international Convention for the Suppression of the Traffic in Persons [and of the Exploitation of the Prostitution of Others] from 1949 had already called on all states to suppress prostitution. . . .

Others disagree. They argue that the legalization of prostitution will improve working and safety conditions for sex workers, allowing sex businesses to recruit among domestic women who choose prostitution as their free choice of occupation. This, in turn, makes resorting to trafficked women less attractive. While those who call for combating prostitution with the force of the law typically subscribe to the belief that prostitution is almost always forced and rarely truly voluntary, the view that the legalization of prostitution may reduce trafficking is typically held by those who believe that the choice to sell one's sexual services for money need not always be forced, but can be a voluntary occupational choice. . . .

A theoretical analysis of the effect of the legality of prostitution on international human trafficking is rendered complicated by the fact that, as [L.] Edlund and [E.] Korn point out, not all prostitution is the same. Street prostitution differs from prostitution in brothels, bars and clubs, which also differs from prostitution offered by call girls (and boys) and escort agencies. Differences include, but are not limited to, the types of services rendered, numbers of clients served, types of clients served, sizes of payments and also the share of illegally trafficked prostitutes working in each market segment. For simplicity, we will avoid such complications by assuming that there is one single market for prostitution.

Let us assume a situation in which prostitution is entirely illegal in a country and those engaging in prostitution—i.e., sex workers, their pimps and clients—are prosecuted, if caught. As with other illegal markets, e.g., the market for classified drugs or endangered species, illegality does not eradicate the market, given that there is strong demand from clients on the one hand, and the willingness to supply prostitution services on the other hand. The equilibrium quantity of prostitution will be a function of supply and demand, just as in any other market. A commonly recognized stylized fact is that despite working conditions that many would regard as exploitative, wages earned by prostitutes tend to be high relative to their human capital endowments such as education and skills, and therefore relative to the wages they could earn outside prostitution. This has been explained by factors such as compensation for social stigma and exclusion, risky and unattractive working conditions, and forgone marriage benefits. Another reason, we suggest, is the compensation for allowing random and often previously unknown clients to infiltrate private and intimate spheres. Importantly, there will be a wage premium, all other things being equal, if prostitution is illegal compared to a situation in which prostitution is legal, since sex workers (and their pimps) need to be additionally compensated for the risk of prosecution. This is similar to the price premium for banned goods like drugs.

What will be the effect of legalizing prostitution on the demand, supply, and thus equilibrium quantity of prostitution? Starting with the demand effect, some clients will be deterred from consuming commercial sex services if prostitution is illegal and they expect that there is a reasonable probability of being prosecuted, as this raises the costs of engaging in such activities. Legalizing prostitution will therefore almost invariably increase demand for prostitution. Concerning supply, legalizing prostitution will induce some potential sex workers (or their pimps) to enter the market, namely those who were deterred from offering such services by the threat of prosecution and for whom the pay premium that arose from the illegality of prostitution represented insufficient compensation—i.e., the risk of prosecution creates costs that are not easily expressed in monetary terms and can therefore not be compensated for with a higher wage. One might conjecture that supply could also decrease given that the state will want to raise taxes from legalized prostitution, whereas illegal prostitution, by definition, does not entail payment of taxes. However, this is not the case. Those unwilling or unable to operate legally (including meeting the legal obligation to pay taxes), can continue to operate illegally. Before, their business was illegal because prostitution was illegal; now their business is illegal due to their tax evasion in the shadow economy. Supply could only decrease under the assumption that the state prosecutes tax evasion more vigorously than it prosecuted illegal prostitution before, which, we believe, will not be the case. As is the case with demand, supply will therefore increase as well. With demand and supply both increasing, the equilibrium quantity of prostitution will be higher in the legalized regime compared to the situation where prostitution is illegal.

If Prostitution Increases, Does Trafficking Increase?

If the scale of prostitution becomes larger once it is rendered legal, will the incidence of human trafficking also increase? The increased equilibrium quantity of prostitution will, for a constant share of trafficked prostitutes among all prostitutes, exert an increasing scale effect on the incidence of international trafficking for prostitution purposes. This is the effect [N.] Jakobsson and [A.] Kotsadam take into account. It is only part of the whole story, however. The full answer to the question depends on what happens to the composition of prostitutes and whether any substitution effect away from trafficked prostitutes (towards domestic prostitutes or foreign prostitutes legally residing and working in the country) is stronger than the scale effect. Under conditions of illegality, a certain share of prostitutes will consist of trafficked individuals, given the difficulties in recruiting individuals willing to voluntarily work in such an illegal market. This share of trafficked prostitutes is likely to fall after legalization. Sex businesses wishing to take advantage of the legality of prostitution (instead of remaining illegal) would want to recruit more national citizens or foreigners legally residing with a work permit in the country since employing trafficked foreign prostitutes (or, for that matter, illegally residing foreign prostitutes that were not trafficked) endangers their newly achieved legal status.

However, the legalization of prostitution will not reduce the share of trafficked prostitutes to zero. First, there may be insufficient supply among domestic or legally residing foreign individuals, given the risky and unattractive nature of prostitution which persists even after legalization. Second, trafficked individuals are significantly more vulnerable and exposed to the demands of their pimps, which makes their continued employment attractive to some extent. For example, a greater portion of their earnings can be extracted, making their pimps' business more lucrative than operating with legal prostitutes. Third, clients might have preferences for "exotic" sex workers from geographically remote places whose nationals are unlikely to have legal rights to reside in the country.

Case Studies

Our empirical findings so far indicate that the scale effects of the expansion of prostitution markets after legalization dominate the substitution effects away from human trafficking. However, our quantitative empirical analysis is cross-sectional. As pointed out already, this means we cannot control for unobserved country heterogeneity. Also, while we have established that the legalized status of prostitution is associated with a higher incidence of trafficking inflows, a cross-sectional analysis cannot provide a conclusion as to whether legalizing prostitution would result in increased trafficking after legalization. In order to provide anecdotal evidence that our estimated effect of legalized prostitution is likely to capture a causal rather than a spurious effect, we now briefly analyze three country case studies, namely Sweden, Germany and

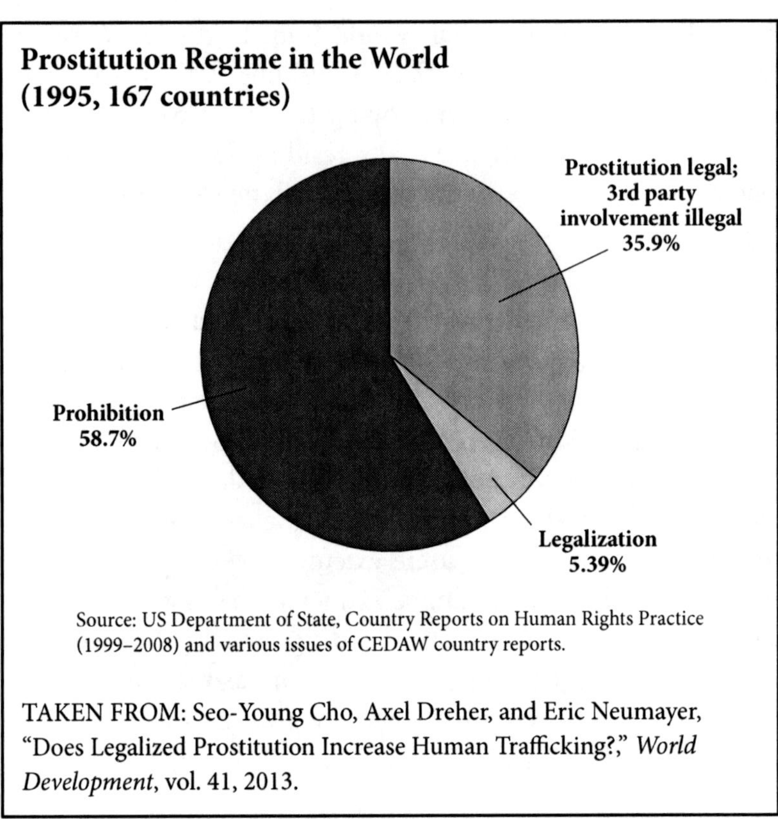

Prostitution Regime in the World (1995, 167 countries)

Source: US Department of State, Country Reports on Human Rights Practice (1999–2008) and various issues of CEDAW country reports.

TAKEN FROM: Seo-Young Cho, Axel Dreher, and Eric Neumayer, "Does Legalized Prostitution Increase Human Trafficking?," *World Development*, vol. 41, 2013.

Denmark. These three countries changed their prostitution law during the 1996–2003 period our investigation covers, albeit in opposite directions. Sweden prohibited prostitution in 1999, while Germany further legalized prostitution by allowing third-party involvement in 2002. Denmark, where prostitution as a main income source was previously illegal, decriminalized prostitution in 1999. Since then, self-employed prostitution is legal but brothel operation is still forbidden in Denmark.

We have sufficient data for Germany to compare the number of trafficking victims in the pre- and post-legalization period. For Sweden and Denmark, we lack such data. We therefore compare the available data for Sweden after the prohibition of prostitution with data for Denmark, where prostitution was legalized. Sweden and Denmark have similar levels of economic and institutional development, and a similar geographic position, which, as our quantitative analysis shows, are important determinants of human trafficking.

Sweden amended its prostitution law in 1999 by prohibiting all forms of commercial sex and punishing the purchase of sex with a fine or imprisonment for a maximum of six months. Prior to the amendment, Sweden allowed self-employed individual prostitution while prohibiting brothel operation. The amendment was introduced after long debates over the root causes of prostitution in Swedish society, with the new law stating that prostitution by nature is always exploitative, and that the purchase of sexual services provided by women and girls amounts to discrimination against them. Furthermore, this new law links prostitution to human trafficking and specifically states the former as an alleged cause of the latter. [G.] Ekberg estimates—based on various cases reported to the Swedish Ministry of Industry, Employment, and Communications—that the number of prostitutes in Sweden decreased rather substantially from 2,500 in 1999 to 1,500 in 2002, with street prostitution in particular decreasing by between 30–50% after the prohibition of prostitution. At the same time, Ekberg points out that even though so-called 'hidden prostitution' via Internet and escort services may have increased, it is generally agreed that the prostitution market in Sweden contracted after prohibition, as a buyer now risks facing criminal charges for purchasing sex. Such evidence of a shrinking market indicates that the prohibition of prostitution in this particular case has a negative scale effect on prostitution markets, as theory predicts.

However, whether or not human trafficking inflows have reduced after the prohibition in Sweden is a trickier question to answer because of the lack of sufficient time-series data on the number of victims. [A.] Di Nicola et al. provide annual estimates of human trafficking victims for sexual exploitation in Sweden during the 2000–03 period, suggesting anywhere between 200 to 600 victims per year. This would mean a share of trafficked individuals among the estimated 1,500 prostitutes of between 13.3% and 40%. There are, however, no available nationwide statistics on trafficking victims prior to the amendment in 1999 and therefore, a direct comparison between the pre- and post-prohibition periods is impossible. However, for the substitution effect to dominate the scale effect, as well as for the number of trafficked prostitutes to have been higher after prostitution was rendered illegal, it would need to be shown that the share of trafficked prostitutes was less than 8% at the minimum estimate, or 24% at the maximum estimate of 2,500 prostitutes prior to 1999. A compositional shift from 13.3% to 8% (minimum estimate) or from 40% to 24% (maximum estimate) is of course possible, but would appear to require quite a large shift.

Sweden and Denmark

A comparison between Sweden and Denmark, a neighboring country with similar socioeconomic conditions yet reforming their prostitution laws in the opposite direction, tentatively suggests that compositional differences across regimes legalizing and prohibiting prostitution have been small. Since 1999, Denmark has allowed individual, self-employed prostitution, while prohibiting brothel operation, representing the same level of legality in prostitution as Sweden had before the 1999 reform. The ILO [International Labour Organization] estimates the stock of human trafficking victims in Denmark in 2004 at approximately 2,250, while the estimated number in Sweden is about 500 (global report data used in [G.] Danailova-Trainor and [P.] Belser, 2006). This implies that the number of human trafficking victims in Denmark is more than four times that of Sweden, although the population size of Sweden (8.9 million) is about 40% larger than that of Denmark (5.3 million). Importantly, the global report also estimates the number of prostitutes in Denmark—about 6,000—to be three to four times larger than the number in Sweden. This comparison thus tentatively suggests that the share of trafficked individuals among all prostitutes is fairly similar in the two countries, despite one prohibiting and the other permitting prostitution. This in turn, would suggest that compositional changes and thus the substitution effect are likely to have been small.

Contrary to Sweden, Germany introduced a more liberal prostitution law in 2002. Today, prostitution in Germany is regulated by law and regarded as a 'regular job' subject to tax payment and retirement schemes. Prior to 2002, Germany only allowed individual, self-employed prostitution without third-party involvement. Having a liberal prostitution regime, Germany is known to have one of the largest prostitution markets in Europe, with about 150,000 people working as prostitutes (global report data used in Danailova-Trainor and Belser, 2006). This means that the number of prostitutes in Germany is more than 60 times that of Sweden, while having a population (82 million inhabitants) less than 10 times larger. In terms of human trafficking victims, the ILO estimated the stock of victims in Germany in 2004 to be approximately 32,800—about 62 times more than in Sweden (Danailova-Trainor & Belser, 2006). Again, the share of trafficked individuals among all prostitutes appears to be quite similar in both countries, corroborating the view that any compositional differences across prohibitionist and legalized prostitution regimes are likely to be small. Additionally, Di Nicola et al. provide annual estimates of trafficking victims used for sexual exploitation in Germany over the 1996–2003 period, which can shed some light on the changing number of trafficked prostitutes. The estimates show that the number of victims gradually declined between 1996/97, the first years of data collection, and 2001, when the minimum estimate was 9,870 and the maximum 19,740. However, this number increased upon fully legalizing prostitution in 2002, as well as in 2003, rising to 11,080–22,160 and 12,350–24,700, respectively. This is consistent with our result from the quantitative analysis indicating a positive correlation between the legal status of prostitution and inward trafficking.

Legalization Leads to More Trafficking

This [viewpoint] has investigated the impact of legalized prostitution on inflows of human trafficking. According to economic theory, there are two effects of unknown magnitude. The scale effect of legalizing prostitution leads to an expansion of the prostitution market and thus an increase in human trafficking, while the substitution effect reduces demand for trafficked prostitutes by favoring prostitutes who have legal residence in a country. Our quantitative empirical analysis for a cross-section of up to 150 countries shows that the scale effect dominates the substitution effect. On average, countries with legalized prostitution experience a larger degree of reported human trafficking inflows. We have corroborated this quantitative evidence with three brief case studies of Sweden, Denmark and Germany. Consistent with the results from our quantitative analysis, the legalization of prostitution has led to substantial scale effects in these cases. Both the cross-country comparisons among Sweden, Denmark and Germany, with their different prostitution regimes, as well as the temporal comparison within Germany before and after the further legalization of prostitution, suggest that any compositional changes in the share of trafficked individuals among all prostitutes have been small and the substitution effect has therefore been dominated by the scale effect. Naturally, this qualitative evidence is also somewhat tentative as there is no "smoking gun" proving that the scale effect dominates the substitution effect and that the legalization of prostitution definitely increases inward trafficking flows. The problem here lies in the clandestine nature of both the prostitution and trafficking markets, making it difficult, perhaps impossible, to find hard evidence establishing this relationship. Our central finding, i.e., that countries with legalized prostitution experience a larger reported incidence of trafficking inflows, is therefore best regarded as being based on the most reliable existing data, but needs to be subjected to future scrutiny. More research in this area is definitely warranted, but it will require the collection of more reliable data to establish firmer conclusions.

The likely negative consequences of legalized prostitution on a country's inflows of human trafficking might be seen to support those who argue in favor of banning prostitution, thereby reducing the flows of trafficking. However, such a line of argumentation overlooks potential benefits that the legalization of prostitution might have on those employed in the industry. Working conditions could be substantially improved for prostitutes—at least those legally employed—if prostitution is legalized. Prohibiting prostitution also raises tricky "freedom of choice" issues concerning both the potential suppliers and clients of prostitution services. A full evaluation of the costs and benefits, as well as of the broader merits of prohibiting prostitution, is beyond the scope of the present [viewpoint].

Viewpoint

> *"What is misleadingly called the 'legalization' of prostitution is actually the recognition of sex work as labor."*

Legalizing Sex Work Does Not Increase Sex Trafficking

Matthias Lehmann and Sonja Dolinsek

Matthias Lehmann is an independent German researcher based in Berlin. Sonja Dolinsek is a graduate student in contemporary history and philosophy at Humboldt-Universität zu Berlin. In the following viewpoint, they argue that many kinds of prostitution remain illegal in Germany. The failure of German law to protect trafficking victims is not because of legalization, they say, but because of the failures to implement legalization and the poor treatment of trafficking victims. In particular, they note that trafficking victims are often subject to deportation and receive little psychological counseling. Because trafficking victims are disempowered by the German legal system, it is difficult for them to testify against or create strong cases against traffickers, Lehmann and Dolinsek conclude.

Matthias Lehmann and Sonja Dolinsek, "Does Legal Prostitution Really Increase Human Trafficking in Germany?" feministire.com, June 6, 2013.

As you read, consider the following questions:

1. What are some legal restrictions on prostitution in Germany, according to the authors?
2. In the authors' view, why is *Der Spiegel* wrong to point to the case of sixteen-year-old Sina as an instance in which legalizing prostitution has failed a trafficking victim?
3. How do the authors say that Germany should emulate Italy in supporting trafficking victims?

[In the Irish campaign to criminalise sex workers' clients, supporters of this proposal have regularly pointed to the German experience as "proof" of the failure of legalisation—despite the fact that Germany's model is not actually advocated by anyone in the Irish debate. A recent article in the German newspaper *Der Spiegel* appeared to provide support for the view that legalisation has failed, and this has been picked up on and quoted by campaigners for criminalisation in Ireland. In this [viewpoint], translated by the authors from the original German, two Berlin-based researchers explain what *Der Spiegel* got wrong.]

Last week [in June 2013], leading German newsmagazine *Der Spiegel* published a cover story—now published in English—on the alleged failure of the German prostitution law which rendered the state complicit in human trafficking. The deeply flawed report fails, however, to address numerous relevant aspects of human trafficking prevention and prosecution, including victim protection. It also fails to insert much-needed factual evidence into the broader global debate on human trafficking, which is also about labor rights, migration, sustainable supply chains and human rights. *Der Spiegel* thus contributes to a very narrow debate on human trafficking and to the *wrong* debate around sex work.

Our blog post is based on a longer critique published in German on the blog *Menschenhandel Heute*. In this shorter version, we would like to critically engage with the international community on the difficult relationship between trafficking and sex work.

The Myth of Legalization

Prostitution, understood as the selling of sexual services, has been legal in Germany since 1927. In addition, Germany's sex workers have been obliged to pay taxes since 1964. The new prostitution law of 2002 changed some aspects pertaining to the legal relationship between sex workers and clients and some criminal law provisions. It recognized the contract between sex workers and clients as legal and introduced the rights of sex workers to sue clients unwilling to pay for sexual services already provided. In addition, sex workers received the right to health insurance and social security. The law also forbids the right of direction (*Weisungsrecht*) by the employer in cases where a sex worker is employed at a brothel, for instance. In this way, a sex worker would always be able to determine to which sexual practices she or he would agree or not. What is misleadingly called the "legalization" of prostitution is actually the recognition of sex work as labor.

However, the law has encountered opposition in the implementation process. Rather than the law itself, as *Der Spiegel* claims, it is the unwillingness of some German states to correctly implement the law. Germany's federal structure requires every state to issue its own implementation directives, which, as political science professor Rebecca Pates explains, did not happen in states like Bavaria or Saxony. Pates argues that some states actually never implemented the new law due to moral reservations with regard to prostitution. . . . Other researchers presented similar findings. Her claims are supported by an official government report of 2007, which identifies the political unwillingness to implement the law as a reason for its failure. *Der Spiegel*'s analysis ignores this fact.

Technically speaking, prostitution is not legal everywhere in Germany. Most states prohibit prostitution in areas close to schools, churches, hospitals or residential areas, and most cities have defined restricted areas (*Sperrbezirke*) and times, where and when prostitution is not allowed. Some cities declare the whole city a restricted area, mostly with the exception of dark and dangerous outskirts, or allow prostitution only during the night. Furthermore, most states prohibit prostitution in cities with less than 30,000 inhabitants. This makes prostitution *de facto* illegal in most places and at most times, and sex workers receive fines or jail sentences if they violate the restrictions. In addition, sex work is not allowed for non-EU [European Union] nationals (third country nationals), who would breach their residency requirements, if they engaged in prostitution. Non-EU nationals engaging in sex work are thus criminalized and made vulnerable not *by* the law, but because they are *excluded* from the law. Therefore, the incomplete legalization of prostitution may be the actual reason why the German prostitution law is failing its purpose to protect sex workers on the one hand, and why, on the other hand, most victims of human trafficking are from third countries.

"Pimping" in Germany and the War with Numbers

New criminal law provisions were introduced with the reform. As *Der Spiegel* correctly points out, the criminal offence "promotion of prostitution" was replaced with "exploitation of prostitutes." In his response to the *Spiegel*'s cover story, Thomas Stadler, attorney at law, explains:

> 'The claim that procuration would only then be a criminal offence if it was "exploitative" or "organized in a dirigiste manner", which is hardly verifiable, is tendentious, at the very least. According to prevailing legal norms, those activi-

ties are deemed as procuration ("pimping") where someone exploits a person that works as a prostitute, controls this person's work to gain pecuniary advantages, dictates the place, time, degree or other circumstances of this work or takes measures to prevent this person from exiting prostitution that go beyond an isolated incidence. Insofar, there might be individual cases, just as in other criminal proceedings, where evidence is hard to come by. One has to ask, however, what procuration actually is and how the legislator is supposed to define it. According to previous legal norms, cases could be built on the establishment of a pleasant atmosphere, which rendered virtually anyone a "pimp" that had some sort of function in a prostitute's orbit. The decrease in convictions might therefore result from the removal of juridical measures that were questionable in the first place. And that surely wouldn't be a step backwards.'

In addition, the new criminal offence of "human trafficking for sexual exploitation" was introduced. As Stadler points out:

> Human trafficking is certainly a criminal offence. In §232 StGB, the criminal code even contains its own article that deals with human trafficking for the purpose of sexual exploitation. The level of the penalty ranges between six months and 10 years. Introduced in 2005, this article is a considerable increase from the previous regulation, §180b StGB, both with regards to content and the penalty range. Since this article includes the so-called "forced prostitution", the actual topic of the *Spiegel* article, the message of *Der Spiegel*'s cover is entirely incorrect. A sincere report should rather have pointed out that the legislator introduced considerably tougher laws to penalize "forced prostitution" in 2005. Therefore, to claim that the state promotes trafficking in women and prostitution is absurd. The opposite is true. The legislator *increased* penalties for "forced prostitution" and human trafficking.

Thus, with a strengthening of labor rights for sex workers came a stronger criminal law, making the exploitation of sex workers as well as human trafficking for sexual exploitation criminal offences.

Der Spiegel suggests that the case of 16-year-old Sina, forced to work in a flat-rate brothel, is a typical example illustrating the failure of the German prostitution law, since the law would not protect her. However, employing a person less than 18 years of age at a brothel is a criminal offence under German law. Thus, Sina's situation is not one that the prostitution law aims to address, and therefore, the law does not fail her in this regard. The failure of the legal system towards her situation and towards other victims of exploitation must lie somewhere else.

Contrary to *Der Spiegel*, the number of convictions for "pimping" did neither decrease nor increase in statistically significant ways with the new law. *Der Spiegel* claims 32 identified "pimps" were convicted in 2011, as opposed to 151 in 2000. An official government reply to a parliamentary enquiry from 1997, however, shows that low convictions for "pimping" were actually a trend: in 1994, there were only 39 convictions for "pimping." Numbers from the federal statistics bureau suggest similar developments.

According to official statistics, the number of officially identified victims of human trafficking decreased significantly in the past fifteen to twenty years. The same government reply from 1997 mentioned 1,196 victims of human trafficking in 1995 and 1,473 victims in 1996, while the statistics of the past four years on record show steady figures of an annual 610 to 710 victims of human trafficking for sexual exploitation, i.e., 640 victims in 2011.

Human trafficking for labor exploitation is also a criminal offence, which so far has failed, however, to attract much interest by the German public. Recent research has shown that, until recently, even counseling centers for victims of human trafficking were mostly unaware of the possibility of labor trafficking and unprepared to provide adequate support. The general lack of interest towards labor trafficking is reflected in the low number of identified victims: only 32 individuals in 2011.

So, Where Is the Real Problem?

Der Spiegel's greatest omissions are victim protection and victims' rights when it comes to human trafficking. A narrow focus on the prostitution law and sex work prevents the authors from dwelling into the more complex web of legal regulations that make the prosecution of cases of human trafficking difficult in Germany.

First, human trafficking cases are dependent upon the testimony of victims. If they are for some reason unwilling to cooperate with the police and do not wish to testify, their cases will most likely fall apart. Furthermore, psychological support for victims of human trafficking is very limited. In many cases police officers and investigators expect linear and consistent narratives from victims from the very beginning, and utterly fail taking into account any traumas they may have endured just moments before. Victims are therefore not only forced to narrate their experiences over and over again, while their traumas are well and alive, but will also have their credibility judged and refuted as potential witnesses, if for some reason their stories show inconsistencies.

Before we talk about the prostitution law, let's talk about how (potential) victims of human trafficking are treated once encountered by the police, and let's talk about how those practices may in fact reduce to a minimum the willingness to testify.

Second, most victims of human trafficking who are third country nationals or from Romania or Bulgaria are repatriated to their home countries after their testimony. If they do not testify or cooperate with the authorities at all, they will be

History of Prostitution in Germany

A 1999 poll reported that 68 percent of Germans favored legalizing prostitution. This level of support is not unusual in Europe, as majorities in many other nations favor legalization as well. Another survey asked about the acceptability of prostitution, and this poll allows us to compare attitudes before and after legalization in 2002. The proportion of Germans who felt that prostitution can "never be justified" declined from 42 percent in 1981 to 33 percent in 1999, dropping further to 24 percent in 2005—a trend toward greater tolerance that may have been catalyzed by legal reform in 2002.

Prior to 2002, selling sex was not a crime in Germany, nor was operating a brothel. But court rulings considered prostitution to be immoral and antisocial, and prostitutes had virtually no rights. It was a crime for third parties to be involved in "the furtherance of prostitution"—for example, pimping, promoting, and profiting from prostitution. This did not apply to brothel owners as long as they did not keep workers in a state of dependency, meaning any action that went beyond providing accommodation (although in practice these owners operated in some jeopardy of violating the "furtherance" measure).

Ronald Weitzer,
Legalizing Prostitution: From Illicit Vice to Lawful Business.
New York: New York University Press, 2012.

deported immediately after a reflection period of three months. Many decry the unwillingness of victims to testify as one central reason for the failure of trafficking prosecution. So far, however, little has been done to encourage testimony and cooperation by strengthening victims' rights. What *Der Spiegel* fails to understand is that a reform of the prostitution law would have no impact on this aspect whatsoever. By focusing on the victims, the authors risk tapping into a dangerous rhetoric of victim blaming, and thus miss how not the prostitution law but the German immigration law actually contributes to much of the vulnerability of migrant women who are victimized. Germany should rather look towards Italy, where victims of human trafficking are unconditionally granted a residency permit and can begin rebuilding their lives.

Last but not least, Germany and the German media have so far missed the opportunity to broaden the public debate on human trafficking and modern slavery to include labor trafficking, organ trafficking as well as labor exploitation in supply chains of large corporations. Instead, the term human trafficking is often equated with prostitution by the media, politicians and even activists, thus perpetuating a selection bias towards women in the sex industry. Victims of other genders or in other sectors run not only a very high risk of never being detected but also of not even being believed. In this sense, we believe *Der Spiegel* has failed its declared commitment towards human trafficking victims—as the majority are conveniently left out, while others, like self-determined (migrant) sex workers, simply are not victims of trafficking.

The Story and Representation of Carmen, a Sex Worker from Berlin

The German print version of *Der Spiegel*'s cover story also featured an inset profile about Carmen, a sex worker from Berlin. Carmen works as an escort as well as a sex workers' rights activist, a role she also fulfills as member of the German Pirate Party. She reacted to the profile by publishing a counterstatement, in which she quoted the email exchange with *Der Spiegel*'s journalist prior to the interview and publication. Contrary to the agreed terms, Carmen writes, the profile dealt only marginally with her "thoughts about prostitution policies, the sex workers' rights movement, the discrimination of sex workers" or other relevant subjects. Whereas Carmen had agreed to the interview to introduce "arguments instead of prejudices into the public debate about prostitution and allow insights into an occupation that most people have no access to," 80 per cent of the eventual profile contained stereotypical descriptions of Carmen's appearance and her escort website.

"I am not prepared to be made a projection screen of any clichés. I will not answer any personal questions that concern aspects outside my work in prostitution/politics," Carmen had written prior to the interview.

In addition, *Der Spiegel* had altered the photo that Carmen had provided to be featured. While blackening her face without her consent anonymized her, the color corrections effectively highlighted her décolleté, further adding to the overall tone of the article.

After Carmen's statement had gone viral, the journalist published his own counterstatement on *Der Spiegel*'s blog, only to draw more criticism. Under the headline "An Escort Lady Makes Politics: Be Truthful," he admitted the non-consensual alteration of the image but claimed it was done to protect Carmen's privacy, even though she had not explicitly asked for any such changes. Where the article's focus and tone were concerned, he invoked the freedom of the press.

Interestingly, *Der Spiegel* also tried to do damage control by sending customized tweets to those who had twittered Carmen's statement, and for its international online publication, *Der Spiegel* then chose to *omit* Carmen's profile entirely, thus removing the one voice, if poorly presented, opposing the cover story's narrative that legalizing prostitution in Germany had failed.

Der Spiegel also published a photo series to support the article's narrative, which included voyeuristic images, a photo of Christine Bergmann, federal minister of family affairs when the German prostitution law was passed (of whom no other picture seemed available as that in front of a sign about child abuse), an angelic picture of Swedish anti-prostitution activist Kajsa Ekis Ekman, and to counter that, an unflattering photo of Volker Beck, human rights spokesperson of the German Greens and a staunch supporter of sex workers' rights.

Viewpoint 3

> *"The most promising method of decriminalizing victims of sex trafficking implemented thus far is the so-called 'Nordic model.'"*

The Nordic Model Can Protect Trafficking Victims

Michelle Madden Dempsey

Michelle Madden Dempsey is a law professor at Villanova University. In the following viewpoint, she argues that criminalizing sex trafficking victims is morally wrong and violates international law. Decriminalizing the entire sex industry, she argues, tends to cause an increase in sex trafficking. Therefore, the best option is to follow the Nordic model, which criminalizes the purchase of sex rather than the people offering sexual services. The Nordic model, she concludes, has reduced prostitution and sex trafficking in areas where it has been used and should therefore be adopted by the United States.

As you read, consider the following questions:

1. What international laws require the United States to decriminalize sex trafficking victims, in Dempsey's view?

2. What does Dempsey believe is wrong with Minnesota's safe harbor law for child victims of sex trafficking?
3. What statistics does Dempsey cite to show a decrease in prostitution in Sweden under the Nordic model?

Despite the United States' commitment to decriminalizing victims of sex trafficking and the obvious injustice of subjecting these victims to criminal penalties, the majority of jurisdictions throughout the U.S. continue to treat sex trafficking victims as criminals. This [viewpoint] argues that the criminal law must abandon this practice. . . .

Penalizing Victims

Generally speaking, a properly functioning criminal justice system spends most of its resources targeting those who victimize others, and aims to provide some measure of protection, vindication, or at least expressive support to those who are victimized. No matter what the resolution to debates regarding whether any so-called "victimless crimes" may justifiably be criminalized, the following remains true: In cases where someone *is* indeed victimized, the criminal law should generally seek to punish the victimizer, not the victim.

These general observations regarding the proper function of the criminal justice system, while uncontroversial, have not held true when it comes to sex trafficking. Instead, the criminal law has too often been used to penalize victims, rather than penalizing those who victimize them. Specifically with regard to criminal laws prohibiting prostitution and related activities such as solicitation, police and prosecutors have spent far more time and money targeting those who sell sex, often under conditions amounting to sex trafficking, rather than targeting those who profit from or drive demand for the commercial sex markets in which trafficking takes place.

While this situation is beginning to change in some states and localities within the United States, the vast majority of jurisdictions continue to criminalize victims of sex trafficking. Despite the U.S. having ratified international agreements requiring the decriminalization of sex trafficking victims, thirty-two states within the U.S. continue to treat child victims as criminals, and no states have comprehensively decriminalized adult victims of sex trafficking.

The continued criminalization of sex trafficking victims in the United States is a tragedy, an embarrassment, and a breach of our obligations under international law. The future of criminal law in this country must confront this issue and move swiftly toward decriminalizing victims of sex trafficking. This [viewpoint] provides a road map for doing so, by identifying what counts as sex trafficking, explaining why we should decriminalize its victims, and outlining four methods for so doing. . . .

Why We Should Decriminalize Victims of Sex Trafficking

A. Our Obligations Under International Human Rights Law May Require It. One reason why criminal justice systems within the U.S. should decriminalize victims of sex trafficking is that our failure to do so likely violates our obligations under international human rights law. Indeed, in a recent review of the U.S.'s compliance with our treaty obligations under the International Covenant on Civil and Political Rights (I.C.C.P.R.), the U.N.'s Human Rights Committee expressed concern regarding the U.S.'s continued criminalization of victims of sex trafficking on prostitution-related charges. The committee criticized our current practices and directed the U.S. to "take all appropriate measures to prevent the criminalization of victims of sex trafficking." As Cynthia Soohoo, director of the International Women's Human Rights Clinic at the City University of New York School of Law observed, the committee sent "a clear message that criminalizing trafficking victims violates their fundamental human rights."

In addition to our obligations under the I.C.C.P.R., our status as a state party to the Palermo protocol grounds further obligations that are, at best, inconsistent with the U.S.'s current practice of criminalizing victims of sex trafficking. For example, the stated purpose of the protocol, set forth in article II, includes the explicit aim "to protect and assist the victims of such trafficking, with full respect for their human rights." Moreover, article VI of the protocol establishes a series of obligations regarding "[a]ssistance to and protection of victims of trafficking in persons." While the protocol does not specifically prohibit criminalization in particular cases, the U.S.'s widespread failure to identify victims of sex trafficking, which results in their continued, indiscriminant criminalization, is surely inconsistent with the commitment "to assist and protect victims . . . with full respect for their human rights."

B. We Tell Other Countries to Do It. Another strong reason weighing in favor of decriminalizing victims of sex trafficking throughout the U.S. is that we hold ourselves out as the "global sheriff" on trafficking, demanding that other countries refrain from criminalizing victims in their own criminal justice systems. For nearly fifteen years, the U.S. has served as the world's most powerful monitor of trafficking in persons, with the annual publication of the "Trafficking in Persons Report" (TIP Report). The TIP Report ranks countries throughout the world on a multi-tier system, according to their compliance with "minimum standards for the elimination of trafficking in persons." If countries rank highly, they remain in good standing with the U.S. and receive our praise for appropriately tackling human trafficking. If countries rank poorly, they face a range of negative consequences, including the imposition of unilateral sanctions by the U.S.

Amongst the many criteria used to assess whether a government has satisfied the "minimum standards for the elimination of human trafficking," one speaks directly to the decriminalization of trafficking victims. Specifically, the U.S.

calls upon other countries to "ensure[] that victims are not inappropriately incarcerated, fined, or otherwise penalized solely for unlawful acts as a direct result of being trafficked." Thus, if a foreign country were to arrest and prosecute a sex trafficking victim for prostitution or solicitation, that country would fail to comply with the "minimal requirements for the elimination of human trafficking" set forth in the TIP Report. And yet, throughout most jurisdictions in the U.S., sex trafficking victims continue to be incarcerated, fined, and otherwise penalized for the very same types of offense.

While the U.S. federal government encourages U.S. states and localities to identify and decriminalize sex trafficking victims, the widespread failure of state and local governments to do so results in the U.S. failing to comply with the "minimal requirements for the elimination of human trafficking" articulated in its own TIP Report. The continued criminalization of sex trafficking victims throughout many states and localities within the U.S. results in a situation in which our federal government, holding itself out as "global sheriff" to the world, hypocritically demands a level of compliance from foreign countries that it cannot effectively require within its own borders. Thus, to put an end to this global hypocrisy, state and local governments throughout the U.S. must stop criminalizing sex trafficking victims for prostitution-related offenses.

Criminalization and Blameworthiness

Those who support criminal laws prohibiting the sale of sex have traditionally sought to justify such laws on grounds of public morality and nuisance. This [viewpoint] will explain why neither of these rationales provides an adequate justification for criminalizing sex trafficking victims, and why sound principles of criminalization weigh in favor of decriminalizing these victims.

Until recently, prostitution was largely viewed as a victimless crime—one that was prohibited primarily because the majority of the voting public viewed the conduct as immoral. As a matter of U.S. constitutional law, however, such a rationale is no longer an adequate justification for criminalization. For, as Justice [Anthony] Kennedy confirmed in *Lawrence v. Texas*, "the fact that the governing majority in a State has traditionally viewed a particular practice as immoral is not a sufficient reason for upholding a law prohibiting the practice. . . ." Of course, the privacy-based rationale upon which *Lawrence* struck down anti-sodomy laws does not extend to prostitution-related offenses, and thus *Lawrence* in no way requires that prostitution laws be deemed unconstitutional on privacy grounds. However, the holding in *Lawrence* does limit the range of justifications a state may rely upon in criminalizing conduct. Specifically, post-*Lawrence*, the fact that a practice has been traditionally deemed immoral is not sufficient to justify its criminalization.

Another common justification offered in support of criminalizing prostitution-related activities is that such conduct creates a public nuisance. Yet, when such rationale is applied to people who are selling sex, it primarily targets those who are doing so under conditions that amount to sex trafficking—so-called "street walkers." For these very people—street-level prostitutes—are likely to be subjected to conditions of "force, fraud, or coercion" or the "abuse of power or position of vulnerability" that constitutes their status as victims of sex trafficking. To rely on a public nuisance rationale for criminalizing such people is akin to criminalizing a shooting victim for criminal damage to public property on grounds that his blood stained the public walkway. In both cases, the victims are being criminalized for conduct that results directly from their experience of victimization. The far more just solution to such public nuisance problems, of course, is to target the use of the criminal law toward those who are engaging in victimization, while *de*criminalizing their victims.

In recent years, U.S. society has become increasingly aware that the many people who sell sex are doing so under conditions that amount to trafficking. Moreover, even in those "gray area" cases where reasonable minds may differ regarding whether to characterize a particular case as trafficking, it is rarely if ever the case that the conduct of the prostituted person is sufficiently blameworthy to merit criminalization. As Andrew Simester and Andrew von Hirsch have correctly observed,

> The criminal sanction is the most drastic of the state's institutional tools for regulating the conduct of individuals.... [It] is distinctive because of its moral voice.... Conduct is deemed through its criminalisation to be, and is subsequently punished as, *wrongful* behaviour that warrants blame.
>
> This official moral condemnation ... generates a truth-constraint. When labeling conduct as wrongful, and when labeling those it convicts as culpable wrongdoers, the state should get it right.

Since criminalization expresses moral condemnation, the criminal law should only be used to target those who are morally blameworthy for their conduct. Let us call this the blameworthiness principle. We can apply the blameworthiness principle in discrete cases by asking whether an individual is sufficiently blameworthy for her conduct to merit criminalization. Indeed, such questions should and often do inform prosecutors' decisions regarding whether to pursue criminal charges in particular cases. So, too, can we apply the blameworthiness principle across a range of cases, by asking whether people who engage in that type of conduct are *typically* so blameworthy for so doing that they merit criminalization. This sort of question should and often does inform legislators' decisions regarding whether to criminalize given types of conduct. To be clear, the question legislators should ask themselves is not merely whether people who engage in that type of conduct are sometimes so blameworthy that they merit criminalization, but whether that level of blameworthiness is *typically* present when people engage in that type of conduct.

Applying the blameworthiness principle in the context of criminalizing the sale of sex calls for an evaluation of the conditions under which such conduct typically occurs. If the conditions are such that people who sell sex are typically not so blameworthy as to merit criminalization for their conduct, then they should not be criminalized. While not representing a scientific survey of current views on the matter, to be sure, it is noteworthy that on the popular website "Pro/Con," which tracks public opinion regarding controversial social issues, the only view supporting criminalizing of people who sell sex was grounded in precisely the sort of public morality considerations deemed inadequate to justify criminal penalties in *Lawrence.*

Instead, views in the U.S. have transformed to a point of near universal agreement that selling sex is not so blameworthy as to merit criminalization. On one set of views, selling sex is not wrongful in the first place, and thus it is never the case that those who sell sex are typically so blameworthy as to merit criminalization for so doing. This view is widely shared by those who otherwise find themselves in deep disagreement. For example, both those who view the sale of sex as merely another form of legitimate employment, as well as many who view the sale of sex as a form of discrimination and violence against women, can nonetheless agree that the sale of sex is not so blameworthy as to merit criminalization. On another set of views, even if there is something morally wrong with some or all instances of selling sex, the conditions under which such conduct is commonly performed render the conduct unworthy of blame in the typical case. On either set of views, the criminalization of those who sell sex is unjustifiable under the blameworthiness principle.

Safe Harbor Laws for Children: An Incomplete Solution

One way to decriminalize victims of sex trafficking that is gaining traction in the U.S. is to enact "safe harbor" laws, which call for protection, rather than prosecution, of child victims of sex trafficking. At present, eighteen states have enacted some form of "safe harbor" and thus have begun to move toward decriminalizing this group of victims.

However, this method of decriminalizing victims of sex trafficking remains incomplete in three ways. First, despite the positive steps taken by the eighteen states that have adopted such laws, it remains the case that thirty-two states continue to treat child victims of sex trafficking as criminals. Until such time as every state enacts "safe harbor" laws, child sex trafficking victims in the U.S. will continue to be subjected to criminal penalties. The lack of uniform legal reform to decriminalize child sex trafficking victims is particularly troubling given that pimps and traffickers often transport child victims across state lines for the purpose of commercial sexual exploitation. Thus, for example, a child who may be protected from criminalization for prostitution-related offenses under her home state's "safe harbor" laws may be transported by her pimp to another state to engage in prostitution. If the destination state does not have a "safe harbor" law, the child victim of sex trafficking risks being arrested and prosecuted in the destination state.

Second, several of the "safe harbor" laws that have been adopted thus far are incomplete on their own terms, insofar as they do not necessarily regard all prostituted children under the age of 18 years as victims of sex trafficking. For example, Minnesota's "safe harbor" law . . . contains provisions that continue to allow for the criminalization of child sex trafficking victims between the ages of 16 and 18 years, if the children refuse or fail to complete a diversion program. As one commentator correctly observes,

> This approach fails to respect and protect the human rights of these juveniles as victims, instead implicating them as criminals [who] must take steps to be "better behaved" to avoid an adjudication of delinquency.

The final way in which "safe harbor" laws remain an incomplete method of decriminalizing victims of sex trafficking is that these laws offer no protection for adult victims of sex trafficking. This fact is particularly troubling, given that the majority of victims of sex trafficking were first prostituted as children. Thus, even if a jurisdiction does enact a "safe harbor" law, once a child victim of sex trafficking reaches her 18th birthday, she is no longer offered the protection of these laws, and is instead subject to the full range of criminal penalties for prostitution-related offenses. While "safe harbor" laws are indeed a step in the right direction, much more is needed in order to achieve comprehensive decriminalization of both child and adult victims of sex trafficking.

Screening and Diversion Upon Arrest: Too Little, Too Late

A second method for decriminalizing victims of sex trafficking is to rely on law enforcement officials and/or prosecutors to identify victims and exercise their discretion to decline prosecution. This method, while an improvement over law enforcement strategies that primarily target victims for enforcement action, remains inadequate to address the scope of the problem for two reasons.

First, even with training, there remains too high a risk that law enforcement will fail to identify cases as trafficking when, in fact, the victim is being prostituted under conditions that amount to trafficking. This problem is particularly likely to arise in cases where people arrested for selling sex view themselves as being in a committed domestic relationship with their pimps. If law enforcement officials are looking for evidence of pimping as an indicator of trafficking, they are likely to miss relevant evidence due to the victim's desire to protect her "boyfriend" and her associated lack of self-identification as someone who is being pimped. As Kaethe Morris Hoffer observes based on her extensive work with prostituted women and girls, "A lot of girls and women in the sex trade, if you ask them, 'Do you have a pimp?' they'll say no. . . . But if you ask, 'Do you have a boyfriend to whom you give all the money you make?' they say yes." Moreover, as Kate Mogulescu has observed, "Despite a robust anti-trafficking discourse [in society generally], these notions have not permeated the spheres of urban policing and local criminal courts. Instead, many victims of sex trafficking are arrested and prosecuted for conduct that they are compelled to engage in."

Second, by the time law enforcement is in a position to screen particular cases to determine whether the person who has been arrested for prostitution-related offenses is a victim of sex trafficking, the person is already being subjected to arrest and detention. Given our obligations under international law to refrain from using the criminal law against victims of sex trafficking and our commitment to global norms ensuring that victims "are not inappropriately incarcerated," adopting a method of decriminalization that presupposes that the victim will be arrested and interrogated by law enforcement is a method that does too little, too late.

Decriminalizing Everyone Involved in Commercial Sex: A Failed Experiment

Another method of decriminalizing victims of sex trafficking is to decriminalize everyone involved in commercial sex, including the seller, buyer, pimp, brothel owner, etc. Variations on this approach have been adopted in countries such as the Netherlands, Germany, parts of Australia, as well as in Las Vegas. While levels of attempted regulation vary from place to place, the key similarity is that prostitution and related activi-

The Nordic Countries and Prostitution

Over the last decade, there has been great interest internationally in the development of prostitution policies in the Nordic countries after Sweden, Norway and Iceland introduced general bans against buying sex while it continues to be legal to sell sex in all these countries. In addition, there is a partial ban against buying sex in Finland and a full criminalisation of the purchase of sex is also being debated in Denmark. These legal reforms have come at different times and have, because of this and for other reasons, been influenced by different national and international discourses on prostitution, gender, sexuality, public space, social work, criminal justice, human trafficking and immigration, as well as by welfare state policies. However, they are also related to each other. There are similarities in how the countries define and approach prostitution; the five Nordic countries share general societal developments and there is a strong tradition of regional cooperation, particularly on the issue of prostitution. In the Nordic countries, the issue of prostitution has been high on the public agenda for several decades, and in most debates it is taken for granted that the countries share the goal of wanting to abolish prostitution.

May-Len Skilbrei and Charlotta Holmström,
Prostitution Policy in the Nordic Region: Ambiguous Sympathies. *Farnham, UK: Ashgate, 2013.*

ties are regarded as legitimate forms of work and are not subject to criminalization *qua* prostitution.

This method, while seemingly promising at first glance, fails to provide a plausible solution, for two reasons. First, while it is true that this method does achieve the goal of decriminalizing victims of sex trafficking, it comes with a heavy cost of increasing the overall amount of sex trafficking in the jurisdiction, due to increases in demand for commercial sex that results when prostitution is normalized through legalization. In the most comprehensive empirical study to date on the impact of legalization, researchers from the German Institute for Economic Research, the KOF Swiss Economic Institute, and the London School of Economics and Political Science examined data from 150 countries with a range of policies regarding the legalization or prohibition of prostitution. The study concludes that "countries where prostitution is legal experience larger reported human trafficking inflows," which is to say, legalization of prostitution across the board increases sex trafficking. This result, of course, is not surprising, given the commonsense insight that normalizing prostitution is likely to increase the market demand for commercial sex generally—and that this demand will be met, at least in part, by increasing the total amount of sex trafficking in the jurisdiction. Thus, despite its initial plausibility, the evidence strongly suggests that decriminalizing everyone involved in prostitution simply exacerbates the underlying problem by increasing sex trafficking.

The Nordic Model: Decriminalizing Victims, Without Increasing Trafficking

The most promising method of decriminalizing victims of sex trafficking implemented thus far is the so-called "Nordic model." By decriminalizing people who sell sex and providing comprehensive social support programs for those who wish to exit prostitution, countries such as Sweden, Finland and Iceland have managed to decriminalize victims of sex trafficking, without the unintended effect of increasing the total amount of trafficking that results from legalization of buyers, pimps, etc.

The European Parliament recently endorsed this method of decriminalizing victims of sex trafficking, calling on other European countries to adopt the Nordic model's approach to prostitution. In relevant part, the European Parliament report

> [s]tresses that prostituted persons should not be criminalised and calls on all member states to repeal repressive legislation against prostituted persons;
>
> [c]alls on the member states to refrain from criminalising and penalising prostituted persons, and to develop programmes to assist prostituted persons/sex workers to leave the profession should they wish to do so;
>
> [b]elieves that demand reduction should form part of an integrated strategy against trafficking in the member states.

Research regarding the impact of the Nordic model demonstrates promising results. Prior to its implementation in Sweden (the first country to adopt the model), the Swedish government estimated that "there were approximately 2500 to 3000 prostituted women in Sweden, of whom 650 were on the streets." A large-scale study evaluating the impact of the law, published in 2008, demonstrated a dramatic decrease in the number of people being prostituted in Sweden, estimating that "approximately 300 women were prostituted on the streets" (a decline of more than 50%), while only "300 women and fifty men were found in prostitution being advertised online." While the Nordic model has been criticized on the grounds that it has simply resulted in a shift from street prostitution to Internet-based or "hidden" prostitution venues, "no information, empirical evidence, or other research suggests that this has actually occurred."

Supporters of the Nordic model often invoke additional claims regarding the nature of prostitution, viewing all prostitution as violence against women. Indeed, this view of prostitution has widely informed and motivated the adoption of such laws. Yet, even if one rejects that view, the evidence is clear that the Nordic model achieves two important goals: (1) it decriminalizes victims of sex trafficking for prostitution-related offenses, and (2) it does not result in an increase in the total amount of sex trafficking. On these grounds alone, the Nordic model presents a more attractive option than across-the-board decriminalization of everyone involved in the commercial sex industry discussed above. For, not only does this method achieve the primary goal of removing criminal penalties from victims of sex trafficking, it does not have the unintended consequence of exacerbating the underlying problem by increasing sex trafficking. Moreover, given evidence that adoption of this model has resulted in a dramatic decrease in prostitution in the jurisdictions where it has been adopted, it seems likely that the decrease in prostitution generally has resulted in a concomitant decrease in sex trafficking as well.

The U.S. should decriminalize victims of sex trafficking. Our current practice of arresting and prosecuting victims for prostitution-related offenses is not only a profound injustice, it is likely a violation of our obligations under international law and, at very least, an embarrassing hypocrisy. While some jurisdictions within the U.S. have taken steps toward decriminalizing child victims of sex trafficking, these efforts are inadequate. We should decriminalize all victims of sex trafficking—child and adult—and we should do so in a way that does not result in an overall increase in sex trafficking. In sum, we should adopt a model of prostitution regulation similar to the Nordic model—in which those who sell sex are provided support in exiting the commercial sex trade, while both pimps and buyers face criminal penalties in order to avoid increasing demand.

VIEWPOINT 4

> *"The Swedish Sex Purchase Act is often said to be an effective tool against human trafficking. The evidence for this claim is weak."*

The Nordic Model Does Not Prevent Sex Trafficking and Harms Women

May-Len Skilbrei and Charlotta Holmström

May-Len Skilbrei is a professor at the University of Oslo; Charlotta Holmström is assistant professor at Malmö University. In the following viewpoint, they argue that there is no single Nordic model; the countries of Sweden, Denmark, Norway, Finland, and Iceland all have different laws addressing prostitution, and prostitution law in these countries has not necessarily been a success. Claims that Sweden has reduced prostitution, for example, depend on counts of street prostitution, which has decreased worldwide thanks to the Internet moving sellers indoors. Claims that only buyers are criminalized are also false, as migrant or immigrant women selling sex are still criminalized and often deported. Overall, they say, the Nordic model, to the extent it exists, has not provided many benefits.

May-Len Skilbrei and Charlotta Holmström, "The 'Nordic Model' of Prostitution Law Is a Myth," theconversation.com, December 16, 2013.

As you read, consider the following questions:

1. What do the researchers identify as the differences in prostitution policy between Norway, Sweden, Denmark, Finland, and Iceland?
2. What evidence do the authors present that Sweden's law has not changed perceptions of women who sell sex?
3. According to the viewpoint, what are examples of increased control police exert on prostitution markets?

The "Nordic model" of prostitution is often heralded for being particularly progressive and woman friendly, built on a feminist definition of prostitution as a form of male violence against women. France has moved to adopt a Nordic-inspired approach; policy makers are urging the UK to do the same. But the idea of such a model is misleading, and in no way tells the whole truth about what is going on in the region where it supposedly applies.

There Is No Shared Nordic Model

We recently gave a talk titled "The Nordic Model of Prostitution Policy Does Not Exist." The aim was to provoke reflection and a discussion, but also to tell the truth about prostitution policies in the Nordic countries.

We have researched Nordic prostitution policies since the mid-nineties, and in particular headed a large comparative project on Nordic prostitution policies and markets in 2007–2008. In our work, we examined how Denmark, Finland, Iceland, Norway and Sweden approach prostitution through criminal justice and welfare policies, and reviewed the evidence for how these policies impact Nordic prostitution markets and the people who work in them.

We found that the differences not only between, but also within, the Nordic countries are too great for there to be anything like a shared "Nordic" model—and that the case for their success is far more fraught than popular support would suggest.

Only Sweden, Norway and Iceland have acts unilaterally criminalising the purchase of sex. Finland has a partial ban; Denmark has opted for decriminalisation. The "Nordic model," then, is in fact confined to only three countries.

These countries' laws prohibiting the purchase of sex are often depicted as ways to redistribute the guilt and shame of prostitution from the seller to the buyer of sex. However, this was by no means the only argument for their introduction. Contrary to many common feminist appraisals, these laws do not in fact send a clear message as to what and who is the problem with prostitution; on the contrary, they are often implemented in ways that produce negative outcomes for people in prostitution.

In truth, while these laws have attracted flattering attention internationally, the politics and practices associated with them are very complex. In particular, they are sometimes applied in conjunction with other laws, by-laws and practices specifically aimed at pinning the blame for prostitution on people who sell sex, particularly if they are migrants. For these and other reasons, the Nordic countries' approaches must be judged with caution—and none more so than the most popular example, the case of Sweden.

Where Sweden Leads

Sweden often attracts particular attention in discussions of how to deal with prostitution, not least since reports from the Swedish government conclude that the law there has been a success.

It has often been stated that the number of women in visible prostitution in Sweden has decreased since the Sex Purchase Act (Sexköpslagen) was introduced in 1999; the Swedish police describe the act as an efficient tool for keeping trafficking away from Sweden. The law has broad support among the general public in Sweden, and this has been interpreted as a result of the law having its intended normative effect on opinions of prostitution. But given the available evidence, none of these points is fully convincing.

The claim that the number of people involved in prostitution has declined, for one, is largely based on the work of organisations that report on specific groups they work with, not the state of prostitution more generally: social workers, for example, count and get an impression based on their contact with women in street prostitution in the largest cities. There is no reason to believe that other forms of prostitution, hidden from view, are not still going on.

The oft-cited 2010 Skarhed report [referring to "Evaluating the Swedish Ban on the Purchase of Sexual Services: The Anna Skarhed Report"] acknowledges this—but still concludes that the law is a success based on the number of women in contact with social workers and police. Men involved in prostitution, women in indoor venues, and those selling sex outside the larger cities are therefore excluded from the scope of the report.

This excessive focus on street prostitution handicaps many accounts of the law's implementation, which tend to simply repeat Swedish authorities' claims that the Sex Purchase Act has influenced the size of the prostitution markets. They ignore the fact that since 1999 or so, mobile phones and the Internet have largely taken over the role face-to-face contact in street prostitution used to have—meaning a decline in contacts with women selling sex in the traditional way on the streets of Sweden cannot tell the whole story about the size and form of the country's prostitution markets.

Meanwhile, the Swedish Sex Purchase Act is often said to be an effective tool against human trafficking. The evidence for this claim is weak; Swedish authorities have backed it up with something said in a call intercepted by the police. The official data that does exist is vague; some authors have also pointed out that the act may have raised prices for sex, making trafficking for sexual purposes potentially more lucrative than ever.

There is also scant evidence for the claim that the law has had its advertised effect on the perception of prostitution and people in prostitution. Even though surveys among the general public indicate great support for the law, the same material also shows a rather strong support for a criminalisation of sex sellers. This contradicts the idea that the law promotes an ideal of gender equality: Instead, the criminalisation of sex buyers seems to influence people to consider the possibility of criminalising sex sellers as well. This rather confounds the idea that the "Nordic model" successfully shifts the stigma of prostitution from sex sellers to clients.

Values in Practice

Ultimately, prostitution laws targeting buyers have complex effects on people far beyond those they are meant to target. In addition to this complicating factor, the Nordic countries also police prostitution using various other laws and by-laws. Some of these regulations do, in fact, assume that the women who sell sex are to be punished and blamed for prostitution. This goes to show that one should be careful in concluding that Nordic prostitution policies are guided by progressive feminist ideals, or that they necessarily seek to protect women involved in prostitution. The most telling example of this is the way the Nordic countries treat migrants who sell sex.

In Sweden this is embodied by the Aliens Act, which forbids foreign women from selling sex in Sweden and is used by the police to apprehend non-Swedish or migrant persons suspected of selling sex. This reveals the limits of the rhetoric of female victimisation, with clients framed as perpetrators: If the seller is foreign, she is to blame, and can be punished with deportation.

In Norway, we see similar gaps between stated ideology, written policies, and practice. Even though it is completely legal to sell sex, women involved in prostitution are victims of increased police, neighbour and border controls which stigmatise them and make them more vulnerable. The increased control the Norwegian police exert on prostitution markets so as to identify clients includes document checks on women involved in prostitution so as to find irregulars among them. Raids performed in the name of rescue often end with vulnerable women who lack residence permits being deported from Norway.

Taken together, the Nordic countries' ways of approaching prostitution have been presented nationally and understood internationally as expressions of a shared understanding of prostitution as a gender equality problem, an example of how women's rights can be enshrined in anti-prostitution law. But after looking closely at how the laws have been proposed and implemented, we beg to differ.

VIEWPOINT 5

"When these victims arrive in our courts, even as defendants in criminal cases, it gives us an opportunity . . . to work together to link victims with the services they so desperately need."

New York's Sex Trafficking Courts Will Help Victims

Jonathan Lippman

Jonathan Lippman is chief judge of New York Court of Appeals. In the following viewpoint, he explains that New York State is establishing human trafficking courts. The purpose of these courts is to provide services and counseling to victims of trafficking. In the past, Lippman says, trafficking victims were treated as criminals and revictimized by the justice system. He maintains that the new courts will separate victims from criminals and provide a new template for treating trafficking victims in courts across the nation.

As you read, consider the following questions:

1. According to the viewpoint, where were pilot human trafficking courts established?

Jonathan Lippman, "Announcement of New York's Human Trafficking Intervention Initiative," courtinnovation.org, September 25, 2013. Courtesy of Jonathan Lippman.

2. What evidence does Lippman provide that trafficking is a domestic issue as well as an international one?
3. Besides the trafficking courts, what sort of legislation does Lippman say will help combat trafficking?

New York State chief judge Jonathan Lippman delivered the following remarks at the Citizens Crime Commission [of New York City] on September 25, 2013, announcing the launch of New York's statewide Human Trafficking Intervention Initiative. In New York, human trafficking is largely dominated by the sex trade, and prostitutes are often victims of coercion, neglect, and abuse. Building on pilot programs operating in Queens, midtown Manhattan, and Nassau County that connect those arrested for prostitution to counseling and social services in lieu of jail time, the New York judiciary's initiative represents a significant shift in the way prostitution is viewed by the justice system and communities.

Epidemic of Trafficking

I am delighted to be here at the Citizens Crime Commission's Milstein Policy Forum. I want to thank Richard Aborn and the commission for all of your wonderful work and for inviting me to speak with you this morning. And Richard, it is an absolute pleasure to work with you on so many critical issues facing the criminal justice system. I am here today to talk about what we in the New York judiciary are doing to eradicate the epidemic of human trafficking, which manifests itself most prominently in our state in the form of sex trafficking—a heinous crime where someone profits from forcing a person into prostitution.

Human trafficking is a crime that inflicts terrible harm on the most vulnerable members of society: victims of abuse, the poor, children, runaways, immigrants. It is in every sense a form of modern-day slavery. We cannot tolerate this practice in a civilized society, nor can we afford to let victims of trafficking slip between the cracks of our justice system. Starting today, the New York State court system will undertake an unprecedented statewide initiative to identify trafficking victims, refer them to services, and restore them to law-abiding lives as we confront this horrific practice head-on with all of the resources at our command.

I am announcing, with the collaboration of our justice system partners, the implementation of a comprehensive response to the problem of human trafficking in New York State with the establishment of the Human Trafficking Intervention Initiative. Within the new framework that we are creating, New York will be a trailblazer, the first state in the nation to create a statewide system of courts, designed to intervene in the lives of trafficked human beings and to help them to break the cycle of exploitation and arrest. The human trafficking courts, in urban, suburban, and rural areas throughout the state, will identify appropriate defendants charged with prostitution and related offenses and provide linkages to services that will assist them in pursuing productive lives rather than sending them right back into the grip of their abusers. We estimate conservatively that this new program will open the door for thousands of people to escape a life of abuse and torture.

Victims, Not Criminals

Three pilot courts in Queens, midtown Manhattan, and Nassau County have spearheaded our efforts and are already up and running. By mid-October, locations in every borough of New York City will be operational, and by the end of October, human trafficking courts, stretching from Long Island on the east to Buffalo in the west, will be available to serve trafficking victims—covering close to 95 percent of those charged with prostitution and trafficking-related offenses in our state. By so doing, we embrace an approach to human trafficking that is newly emerging among enlightened criminal justice thinkers around the country who recognize that all defendants are not the same, and that the real perpetrators of crimes are often hidden from view.

Trafficking victims need the kind of resources and services that can transform and save their lives. When these victims arrive in our courts, even as defendants in criminal cases, it gives us an opportunity—an opportunity for judges, prosecutors, and defense lawyers to work together to link victims with the services they so desperately need. This new initiative will stop the pattern of shuffling trafficking victims through our criminal courtrooms without addressing the underlying reasons why they are there in the first place.

Each human trafficking court will have a presiding judge who is trained and knowledgeable in the dynamics of sex trafficking and the support services available to victims. The courts are based on a collaboration among stakeholders working together to identify defendants who have been trafficked. In each of the court locations, we are working to establish new court protocols under the leadership of the court system's chief of policy and planning, Judge Judy Harris Kluger, and her staff. All cases involving prostitution-related offenses will be identified at arraignment and, if not resolved there, be transferred to the local human trafficking intervention court. In the trafficking court, cases will be evaluated by the judge, the defense attorney and the prosecutor and, if there is consensus that the case involves a victim in need of services, appropriate connections will be made. Those who comply with the mandated services will have the opportunity to receive non-criminal dispositions or dismissal of their case. While these prostitution cases are criminal in every sense with all that attends, the human trafficking courts are being established to ensure that there will be no further victimization of these defendants by a society that can be divorced from the realities of this modern-day form of servitude. It is in this context that the new trafficking courts will directly engage the victims of human trafficking through the combined efforts of defense attorneys, prosecutors, legal service providers, law enforcement officials, social services, vocational and educational training providers, domestic violence and sexual assault service providers, and substance abuse and mental health treatment providers.

We know what we are up against. Human trafficking is a multibillion-dollar industry and one that is growing. Among criminal enterprises, it is second only to drug trafficking in profitability. While it is difficult to measure precisely a practice that exists largely in the shadows, the estimates we do have are staggering. According to a recent State Department estimate, across the globe, there are approximately 27 million victims of human trafficking. Of these, as many as 17,500 are brought into the United States. In addition, hundreds of thousands are trafficked within the United States each year. Though human trafficking includes labor trafficking, the vast majority of the victims—nearly 80 percent—are trafficked for sex. Many more victims continue to go uncounted because they are often driven to the margins of our communities, and, as a result, these frightening numbers are almost certainly understated.

A Domestic Issue

Trafficking is as much a domestic issue as it is a transnational one. Around the country, about 80 percent of victims in sex trafficking incidents are U.S. citizens. The great majority of the victims of sex trafficking within the United States are women and children, particularly girls under 18 years of age. Sickeningly, the typical age of entry into prostitution in the United States is only 12 to 14 years old. Many of these victims end up in court as defendants charged with prostitution-related offenses, because they have been induced into illegal conduct. The sad truth is that few of their clients are arrested and even fewer of their traffickers or those who lead them into prostitution are ever charged. They may hesitate to reveal their victimization out of fear or mistrust, and all too often, the players in the justice system are unable to develop a full picture of their circumstances. In the past, victims have easily passed through our criminal justice system without ever being identified as victims of trafficking. But not anymore!

For most of our history, trafficking victims had an entirely negative place in our culture. They were thought of not as victims, but as criminals, addicts, delinquents, incorrigible and profit driven. Many still feel that way, but we have come a long way in our understanding of this complex problem. We have come to recognize that the vast majority of children and adults charged with prostitution offenses are commercially exploited or at risk of exploitation. All too often, they are victims of intimate partner violence, unable to extricate themselves and needing protection from their abusers. They may be runaways, easy prey to traffickers, or be in the grip of an addiction that has led to their exploitation.

In New York, our laws reflect the significant strides that have been taken to address the problem of human trafficking. The New York State anti-trafficking statute, enacted in 2007, created the new state crime of sex trafficking designed to punish those who profit from the sex industry. In 2008, New York's legislature enacted the Safe Harbour for Exploited Children Act, which challenged the legal framework where prostituted children were regarded as criminals. The Safe Harbour Act created a legal presumption that children charged with prostitution were victims of trafficking and mandated that trafficked children under age 16 be treated as persons in need of supervision (PINS) in family court, instead of delinquents. Two years later, New York became the first state in the nation to enact a law allowing judges to vacate convictions for prostitution-related crimes for defendants whose participation in the offense was the result of their having been trafficked. Most recently, the legislature passed a provision extending the Safe Harbour Act to include 16- and 17-year-old victims of trafficking. Under the amended statute, 16- and 17-year-old trafficking victims may also have their case converted to a PINS proceeding instead of being prosecuted for prostitution. New York has a proud history of being a pioneer in this area, and the Trafficking Intervention Initiative I am announcing today ushers in another new chapter in the continued battle to end the ongoing exploitation of these vulnerable individuals.

Systemic Problems, Systemic Response

What we recognize is that a systemic problem such as human trafficking requires a systemic response. The step we take today is comprised of much more than an effort in a limited jurisdiction or by one particular judge to address a sprawling problem, such as has been the case in scattered locales around the country. Our statewide, court-led initiative, informed by our own experience with New York's pilot sites, will address virtually all cases involving trafficking victims in the courts of New York—certainly among the largest and most challenging caseloads in the country—and will incorporate the joint efforts of all of the criminal justice players.

Focusing our efforts on victims of trafficking is only one piece of the larger puzzle. Legislation on the state and federal level has allowed law enforcement to begin to address the root evil that drives the market, the traffickers who exploit these victims and profit from their misery. Though these cases are difficult to investigate and prosecute, each district attorney here, as well as others around the state, is committed to identifying, investigating and bringing charges against the traffickers who operate in their jurisdiction—the people who have made this such a lucrative business undertaking through the exploitation and abuse of the most vulnerable among us—as well as those who pay for sex and feed the demand. By this intense focus on identifying and punishing the real perpetrators of human trafficking and the unflagging commitment that we all pledge today to the just and compassionate resolution of the cases brought against victims, New York will lead the fight against human trafficking.

We are committed to fundamentally changing the way that we as a system think about these cases. In order to do that, we will be providing training on trafficking to our judiciary and court staff across the board. This October, we will convene a day-long training program for judges and their staffs from the new courts that will cover legal topics, best practices from experienced judges, and cultural competency and skills. In addition, we are working with the National Judicial College, the Center for Court Innovation, the Practising Law Institute, and the State Justice Institute to implement broader training to make sure that everyone has an opportunity to deepen their understanding of the tremendously complicated issues facing victims.

In New York, the courts and the justice system will provide a template for the rest of the country in dealing with the societal impact of human trafficking that ultimately ends up in our courtrooms. We in the justice system do not exist in a vacuum separate and apart from such a deep-rooted problem that poisons our communities and our people. We together must be and will be proactive in meeting the challenges that we face from the evil of human trafficking.

I want to recognize the tremendous support of district attorneys, the defense bar, and the service provider community. I commend them for their vision and leadership on this critical issue and thank them for their vital input and participation in this effort. I also want to recognize the many strong voices for change—three of whom I will be introducing shortly—including Kathleen Rice, the president of the District Attorneys Association [of the State of New York]; Steve Banks, attorney in charge of the Legal Aid Society; and Lori Cohen, the director of the anti-trafficking initiative at Sanctuary for Families, who works so closely with its terrific director of legal services, Dorchen Leidholdt. I would note also the Center for Court Innovation for developing responses to trafficking and shining a light on positive innovations, the Judicial Committee on Women in the Courts and its chair Betty Weinberg Ellerin, for its ground-breaking work in this area including the creation of the invaluable "Lawyer's Manual on Human Trafficking," and judicial pioneers like Fernando Camacho, Toko Serita, and so many others.

A Chance to Help

As chief judge, I believe that the courts must play a critical role in reorienting the justice system to more ably serve victims, address public safety concerns, and respond to societal ills. While human trafficking is both complicated and devastating, each case presents us with an opportunity to help. As we have done so often in the past, with drug courts, mental health courts, and others, the court case can be the victim's link to rehabilitation and renewal. With this Human Trafficking Intervention Initiative, we are taking a giant leap forward toward solving this vast and critical problem. For all of us—judges, prosecutors, defense attorneys, legislators, law enforcement, community groups, advocates, and treatment providers—we know that by working together we can change lives, one by one, and be a truly powerful force in combating this scourge of modern society.

Thank you.

Periodical and Internet Sources Bibliography

The following articles have been selected to supplement the diverse views presented in this chapter.

Cedar Attanasio	"Decriminalize Prostitutes, but Not Prostitution, Argues Former U.S. President Jimmy Carter," *Latin Times*, May 19, 2015.
Australian Broadcasting Corporation	"Sweden's So-Called Nordic Model Designed to Protect Sex Workers While Dismantling Their Trade," March 13, 2015.
Elizabeth Nolan Brown	"What the Swedish Model Gets Wrong About Prostitution," *Time*, July 19, 2014.
Naomi Eide and Carly Morales	"Trafficking Victims Lured by Dreams of Better Life," *Star Democrat* (Easton, MD), June 9, 2015.
Jake Flanagin	"What It Takes to Legalize Sex Work," *New York Times*, June 25, 2014.
Rory Lancman	"Trafficking Courts Need More Funds to Aid Victims," *Queens Chronicle* (New York), June 5, 2015.
Liz Robbins	"In a Queens Court, Women in Prostitution Cases Are Seen as Victims," *New York Times*, November 21, 2014.
Joy Smith	"Dear Amnesty International, Legal Prostitution Harms Women," *Huffington Post*, January 31, 2014.
Zach Weissmueller and Will Neff	"Legalize Prostitution to Fight Sex Trafficking? Sex Workers Say 'Yes,'" Reason.com, January 14, 2014.
William Wicki	"Decriminalizing Victims: Let's Adopt the Nordic Model of Prostitution Law," *Stanford Daily*, February 16, 2015.

Chapter 4

How Does Immigration Policy Affect Human Trafficking?

Chapter Preface

In 2015 South Africa introduced new visa rules in part to attempt to regulate immigration and reduce child trafficking. The new rules state that any child crossing South Africa's border must have an unabridged birth certificate. That means that the certificate needs to include the full history of the child, including information on his mother, father, and grandparents. Children traveling without both parents need the missing parent's signature, even in cases of divorce. According to Peggy Drodskie, acting chief executive officer of the South African Chamber of Commerce and Industry, "This unabridged certificate is quite a detailed description of what is required. It's causing big problem[s], furthermore the airline companies are now responsible if a person . . .[should] come into the country and [doesn't] have the entire necessary document, which will mean extra costs for the airline company," she told Thandi Xaba of the News Hub.

The new regulations are supposed to restrict abuse, according to South Africa's home affairs ministry spokesperson Mayihlome Tshwete. "It is common practice for many countries across the world who are trying to make sure the most vulnerable people in our society are protected," he explained to BBC News.

Not everyone in South Africa supports the new regulations. In particular, the tourism industry is very concerned about the effect of tight border restrictions on travel to the country. David Frost, chief executive officer of the Southern Africa Tourism Services Association, explained to Voice of America that "what we are seeing here is akin to taking a sledgehammer to kill a mosquito." Tourism is the fastest-growing part of South Africa's economy, and the new regulations could be devastating. In June 2015, ticketing was already down 20 percent from the previous year. Carriers such as Air

China and Lufthansa reduced flights to South Africa; Frost warned of as many as one hundred thousand job losses.

The South African government believes that thirty thousand children every year are trafficked to South Africa for purposes of forced prostitution or forced labor, though human rights groups put the number substantially lower—perhaps even at only 2 percent of the government figures, or around six hundred children trafficked per year.

If there is not really a serious problem with child trafficking, why the new laws? One possibility is that the restrictions are linked to anti-immigrant sentiment, or a desire to reduce movement across the border. Resentment against immigrants from other African nations led to riots in South Africa early in 2015. The legislation may be more a response to that than to fears about child trafficking.

The following chapter explores how border security and immigration policy may reduce or increase human trafficking.

Viewpoint 1

> *"Most undocumented workers work within a kind of labor purgatory since their exploitation is not exploitative* enough *to qualify as 'trafficking.'"*

Victims of Trafficking Are Defined Too Narrowly, Hurting Immigrants

Denise Brennan

Denise Brennan is chair of the Department of Anthropology at Georgetown University and author of Life Interrupted: Trafficking into Forced Labor in the United States. *In the following viewpoint, she argues that the government tends to define trafficking narrowly to mean only those kidnapped and sexually exploited. At the same time, she says, immigration regulations have been tightened, making it difficult for those who experience abusive working conditions to come forward, for fear of deportation. She concludes that trafficking has been used as a distraction to make anti-migrant and anti-prostitution policies seem altruistic and that US anti-trafficking policies currently increase misery and exploitation.*

Denise Brennan, "Securing Rights and Seeking Justice in the US Deportation Regime," *S&F Online*, Fall 2012/Spring 2013.

As you read, consider the following questions:

1. What does Brennan say defined the Bush administration's understanding of trafficking victims?
2. What are some things that go unreported because of the way immigration policy has terrified and silenced communities, according to Brennan?
3. Why did the United States Conference of Catholic Bishops have their anti-trafficking funding revoked?

A repressive immigration regime premised on raids, arrests, and deportations has profoundly shaped US anti-trafficking policy. Only a small number—under 4,000—of exploited migrants have been assisted by anti-trafficking policies. Meanwhile, vast numbers of migrant workers labor unprotected and live in fear of detection and deportation.

State-Led Assault on Migrants and Sex Workers

Under the rubric of humanitarianism, nation-states single out populations for assistance, but place limits on these commitments, capping how many people they will assist, how much assistance they will provide, and for how long. States establish a hierarchy of recipients using humanitarianism, as anthropologist Didier Fassin writes, as both a "moral discourse" as well as a "political resource" to justify a range of actions. In anti-trafficking humanitarianism, victimhood is bestowed on only a small subset of exploited workers. Trafficked persons worthy of immigration relief and social assistance in the United States are the recipients of a large, government-funded, media-covered, relief apparatus that is disproportionate to the numbers of those actually assisted and of those left to continue working in dangerous and vulnerable situations.

Following the passage of the Trafficking Victims Protection Act (TVPA) in 2000, the [George W.] Bush administration's obsession with prostitution defined its understanding of "trafficking victims," and which organizations would assist with "rescues" and aftercare. The Bush administration decoupled trafficking from the issues of migration and labor, and reframed trafficking as about sex. Fighting trafficking in the United States became a cover for anti-prostitution activists and policy makers to crack down on sex work. The United States' anti-prostitution zealotry had a long reach through the US Department of State's annual "Trafficking in Persons Report" (TIP Report) as well as through US government requirements that any foreign, nongovernmental organizations receiving US government funds for anti-trafficking efforts must sign an anti-prostitution pledge. The stage was set: Trafficking was about coerced sex, a conclusion affirmed by mainstream feminist organizations, evangelical organizations, do-gooder celebrities, and media outlets ready to provide sensationalistic details of sexual sins and redemption.

Almost immediately, the state also undid its own anti-trafficking policies through its immigration policy: First it looked for one kind of trafficking "victim" in brothels and massage parlors, and, in the process, arrested US-citizen sex workers and deported foreign sex workers. By also ramping up immigration raids on workplaces, the state created the current climate of fear of detection. In this environment, abused workers are not coming forward to report actual instances of "trafficking" into forced labor, while migrant women working in the sex sector are coercively "rescued" in the name of ending trafficking. The passage of anti-migrant legislation and policies, on the state and local level, has kept migrant communities distrustful of law enforcement and thus fearful of reporting workplace abuses or crimes in their homes or neighborhoods. These policies also encourage racial profiling. Instead of creating channels of trust and communication, both kinds of raids have had the opposite effect. Not only do exploited workers weigh the risks of reporting abuse, but witnesses to abuse—coworkers, neighbors, and abusers' family members—are not coming forward in this atmosphere of all-out assault on the sex sector and on migrant communities.

Avoiding Detection, Avoiding the State

Between 2005 and 2011, I traveled throughout the United States to meet with individuals whom the US government had determined were "trafficked" to the United States, as part of the field research for a forthcoming book, *Life Interrupted: Trafficking into Forced Labor in the United States* (Duke University Press). My current field research on the effects of deportation—or the threat of deportation—in low-wage communities and work sites grew out of this project with formerly trafficked persons: "exceptions" in this deportation regime. As a scholar-activist on migrants' rights and sex workers' rights, I have been eager to call attention to the vulnerability of large numbers of undocumented—and deportable—migrants. While spectacular stories of women and girls in forced sexual labor dominate in the media and the public's understanding of "trafficking," stories about rampant and unfettered exploitation of migrants in a number of industries go unreported or are taken for granted as part and parcel of doing business.

Although extreme abuse may be exceptional, other forms of exploitation—such as wage theft—are commonplace for migrant workers. Most undocumented workers work within a kind of labor purgatory since their exploitation is not exploitative *enough* to qualify as "trafficking." The new legal relief is a binary regime: one is either trafficked or not. Providing protections for only the most extreme cases of exploitation sidesteps the divisive politics of immigration reform.

In the absence of federal immigration reform, states and localities enacted legislation and ordinances—such as adopting 287(g) agreements [that allow local authorities to perform immigration law enforcement] and "secure communities" programs—that target undocumented migrants. A pediatrician in

Georgia explained the chilling effects of new statewide anti-migrant legislation: "I've never had this happen before. My patients are asking if they should leave Georgia. I do not know what to say to them." The assault on migrants mounts and takes new forms every day. US residents along the US-Mexico border, for example, text Border Patrol agents if they see anyone trying to cross the border. Surveillance by the state—as well as by the ordinary citizenry—has terrified and silenced communities. Extreme vulnerability, exploitation, and violence can result in this environment. Women and men are not reporting domestic violence in their homes and wage theft, unsafe working conditions, sexual assault, or verbal or physical abuses in the workplace.

The violence of the deportation regime is hard to ignore: Nursing mothers have been held in immigration detention and parents have been deported while their US-citizen children stay behind, raised by other family members, friends, or foster care. Individuals in deportation proceedings must report on a regular basis to ICE (US Immigration and Customs Enforcement) subcontractors—immigration "parole officers" of sorts—while waiting for a determination of their legal status. These subcontractors are often hours away—sometimes in another state. It is not only difficult to make ends meet when working part-time to accommodate this parole schedule, but off-the-books employers also know that these employees are in a compromised position to negotiate better pay or work conditions. In these low-wage communities, women often are the main breadwinners in the household since in some local economies they find work in domestic labor or in garment manufacturing more regularly than men looking for work in a flailing construction industry.

Following a raid at a meat-processing plant in Postville, Iowa, 300 of the 389 individuals apprehended by immigration agents were charged, convicted, and sentenced within ten days. Group trials were held in temporary fairgrounds. The Ameri-

Cooperation with Local Law Enforcement: 287(g)

The 287(g) program run by ICE [US Immigration and Customs Enforcement]. . . . extends immigration law enforcement authority by delegating it to state and local law enforcement agencies. States and municipalities that work with ICE through the 287(g) program have their law enforcement officers trained by ICE in immigration enforcement. Agreements vary from checking immigration status of people in local jails to the ability to check the immigration status of anyone detained in the line of work of local police, including routine traffic stops. In this way, many undocumented immigrants are identified, detained, and deported. . . . In 2008, 67 agencies were enrolled in the program. . . .

The Government Accountability Office has criticized the 287(g) program for a lack of internal controls, such as vagueness in program objectives, and for lack of clarity regarding how program authority is to be used, how ICE agents are to supervise cooperating agencies, and what data are to be collected and reported. . . . It undermines community policing that is built on trust between local law enforcement and immigrant communities. If immigrants are afraid that local or state police will check their immigration status and hand them over to ICE, they are much less likely to come forward and report crimes.

Sofya Aptekar,
"Immigration and Customs Enforcement,"
The Making of Modern Immigration:
An Encyclopedia of People and Ideas.
Ed. Patrick J. Hayes. Santa Barbara, CA: ABC-CLIO, 2012.

can Civil Liberties Union observed that the close coordination before the raid between the prosecutor and the chief judge to hasten the process and structure plea agreements was highly irregular and raised due process concerns. While such immigration raids strain notions of justice, the benefits that "trafficked persons" receive expose the contradictory logic that undergirds US immigration policy. Workplace raids, anti-migrant state and local policies, along with ordinary citizens' surveillance, drive undocumented migrants further underground, and anti-trafficking policy collapses in on itself.

The Way Forward for Feminist Politics: Possibilities for Collaborations?

In the struggle to secure migrants' rights and well-being in the United States, activists have faced many setbacks. With the passage of anti-migrant legislation in Arizona (S.B. 1070), and copycat legislation in Alabama, Georgia, Indiana, South Carolina, and Utah, those in the migrants' rights community have been kept running. And, framing trafficking as sex trafficking has rendered workers in the sex sector more vulnerable as they seek to work further underground. It also has hindered progress on preventing forced labor. Time was lost, and critical collaborations between migrants' rights, workers' rights, and sexual rights communities have not been made.

Migrants' rights advocates have strategically avoided collaborations with anti-trafficking advocates, in part to avoid the toxic politics around sexual labor. Sex workers' rights communities have largely been left out of both migrants' rights and anti-trafficking forums and funding. Low-wage workers' rights communities almost never include those working in sexual labor. Just as with issues related to sexual labor, so, too, has the double vulnerability of LGBTI [lesbian, gay, bisexual, transgender, intersex] undocumented community members been left out of discussions on migrants' rights. Certain interest groups—business, political, and religious—benefit from keeping these issues siloed and their advocates working separately. The prisons and detention facilities holding individuals in deportation proceedings are big businesses, with counties throughout the south courting ICE's contracts. Anti-trafficking efforts, popularly understood as "feminist," have provided a smoke screen for anti-prostitution activists to push a range of non-feminist issues. For example, for five years the US government designated the United States Conference of Catholic Bishops (USCCB) as the main contractor to distribute funding for the resettlement of trafficked persons. The revocation of their funding—when it came to light that they had not allowed their subcontractors to provide reproductive health information or services to trafficking clients—has been some good news that bodes well for more evidence-powered policy shifts in the future.

VIEWPOINT 2

> *"From the information available, it appears that the 2008 trafficking law is largely inapplicable to the massive smuggling problem occurring along the U.S. border."*

Victims of Trafficking Are Defined Too Broadly, Creating a Border Crisis

Jon Feere

Jon Feere is a legal policy analyst at the Center for Immigration Studies. In the following viewpoint, he argues that trafficking laws should not apply to many of the children coming across the Mexican border in a large influx in late 2014. He says that many of the children have relatives in the United States, meaning they are not covered by the trafficking law, and many others are not trafficked. He concludes that the trafficking law is being applied too broadly, making it difficult to deal with the influx of illegal immigrants.

As you read, consider the following questions:

1. According to the viewpoint, how does federal law define an unaccompanied alien child?

Jon Feere, "Trafficking Law Largely Inapplicable to Border Crisis," *The Hill*, July 24, 2014.

2. According to Feere, how does the law define a victim of trafficking?
3. What information does Feere say would be helpful in crafting a policy response?

Despite all the attention it has received, the William Wilberforce Trafficking Victims Protection Reauthorization Act of 2008—a law aimed, in part, at "unaccompanied alien children" who are victims of trafficking—appears to have little applicability to the current situation on the border [in which large numbers of children crossed the Mexico border into the United States in late 2014]. As such, the [Barack] Obama administration should not be applying the law and granting protections that are supposed to benefit trafficking victims to people who are willing participants in human smuggling operations. This is an issue I explored in a new report.

Trafficking Law Does Not Apply

There are at least three reasons why the Obama administration is wrong when it asserts that the 2008 trafficking law binds their hands and requires them to grant most young illegal immigrants and their families a day in immigration court, lawyers and other benefits.

First, it appears that a significant majority of children coming across our borders illegally are not "unaccompanied alien children" according to the definition found in federal law. Federal law defines an "unaccompanied alien child" as an illegal alien under the age of 18 who is without "a parent or legal guardian in the United States." Data from government agencies suggest that the overwhelming majority of minors arriving on the U.S. border have family in the United States.

According to advocates and media reports, around 90 percent of non-Mexican and non-Canadian children coming across the border are placed with family or guardians in the United States. Department of Health and Human Services

(HHS) secretary Sylvia Burwell recently testified that approximately 55 percent of released alien children are released to parents and another 30 percent are released to other family members, bringing the total to 85 percent of such children being released to family. Mark Greenberg, acting assistant secretary within HHS, recently testified that, thus far in fiscal year 2014, approximately 95 percent of children released went to a parent, relative or non-relative sponsor. Still, better data from the Obama administration would be helpful.

Willing Participants

Second, there is little evidence that the recent arrivals are victims of trafficking, which generally involves coercion. Instead, families and their children are willing participants in smuggling operations, having paid smugglers to bring them into the United States. As U.S. Immigration and Customs Enforcement explains, "Human trafficking and human smuggling are distinct criminal activities, and the terms are not interchangeable." Yet the aim of the 2008 trafficking law (and related laws) is to prevent people from becoming victims of human trafficking and to protect women and children who are often the targets of human traffickers. The Trafficking Victims Protection Act of 2000 explains that a "victim of trafficking" is a person subjected to an act or practice such as sex trafficking or "involuntary servitude, peonage, debt bondage, or slavery."

While it is likely that some of the illegal immigrants who have recently arrived at the U.S. border were subject to difficult, if not horrific, situations, it is incorrect to refer to them as "victims of trafficking" and apply trafficking laws without evidence that they are, in fact, victims of trafficking.

Third, even if all people coming across the border illegally were "unaccompanied alien children" and victims of trafficking, the 2008 act includes language that gives the president some leeway in its application. The law requires "[e]xcept in the case of exceptional circumstances" that any department or agency of the federal government that has an unaccompanied alien child in custody to transfer the custody of such child to the HHS secretary within 72 hours after determining that such child is, in fact, an unaccompanied alien child. The HHS provides additional benefits to the individuals. Sen. Dianne Feinstein (D-Calif.) recently told Department of Homeland Security secretary Jeh Johnson at a Senate hearing that the "exceptional circumstances" provision would allow President Obama discretion in how the law is applied in light of the current influx of illegal immigration. In other words, the law does not necessarily require that all recently arrived illegal immigrants receive a day in court.

Again, better information about the demographics of people coming across the U.S. border would be helpful in crafting the appropriate political and legal response, but thus far the Obama administration has not been forthcoming with information. From the information available, it appears that the 2008 trafficking law is largely inapplicable to the massive smuggling problem occurring along the U.S. border.

VIEWPOINT 3

"Nepal's struggle with human trafficking has been accentuated by the ten-year civil war between government forces and Maoist rebels that plagued the country from 1996 until 2006."

The Open Border Between Nepal and India Promotes Human Trafficking

Lauren Renda

Lauren Renda is outreach and global connections fellow at Zawadisha and document specialist at the Nevada Legislative Counsel Bureau. In the following viewpoint, she writes that the border between India and Nepal is open, and police coordination across the border is sometimes difficult. This has created a situation in which trafficking of women across the border is rampant and difficult to stop. This problem has been exacerbated by a long civil war that has eroded the rule of law. Many nongovernmental organizations are working to reduce trafficking, and Renda is hopeful they will help contain the problem.

Lauren Renda, "Across the Border: Nepal's Struggle with Human Trafficking," thewip.net, May 25, 2012.

As you read, consider the following questions:

1. According to Renda, what conditions do Nepalese men and women often face when they go to work in the Gulf states?
2. According to the viewpoint, why is WOREC encouraged by the fact that there is a *rise* in reported trafficking cases?
3. According to Renda, what are rates of HIV among Nepalese girls trafficked and rescued from Indian brothels?

Every year thousands of men, women, and children are trafficked from Nepal to India for commercial sexual exploitation, domestic servitude, and bonded labor. Nepal is considered a "source country," or country of origin, where victims are trafficked both within the country as well as to Asian and Middle Eastern destinations.

Forced Labor

With the help of labor brokers and manpower agencies, many young men and women migrate willingly from Nepal to Malaysia, Israel, South Korea, the United States, Saudi Arabia, the UAE [United Arab Emirates], Qatar, and other Gulf states to work as domestic servants, construction workers, or other low-skill laborers. Unfortunately, they are often deceived about their destination, and upon arriving in a foreign country, face conditions indicative of forced labor—the withholding of passports, restrictions on movement, nonpayment of wages, threats, deprivation of food and sleep, and physical and sexual abuse.

Nepal's struggle with human trafficking has been accentuated by the ten-year civil war between government forces and Maoist rebels that plagued the country from 1996 until 2006. During this time, lawlessness and violence were rampant. Today, even after the conflict's end, the country faces a severe lack of rule of law, impunity, and blanket amnesty for perpetrators of war crimes and human rights violations. While steps have been made to quell human trafficking, without an effective government in place, it has been complicated. With pressure from the United Nations, Nepal was one of 117 countries to sign the Protocol to Prevent, Suppress and Punish Trafficking in Persons, Especially Women and Children (the Trafficking Protocol), adopted by the United Nations in 2000. It is the first global, legally binding instrument on trafficking. Nepal's [Human] Trafficking and Transportation (Control) Act of 2007 was expected to solve the problem of human trafficking by laying out and enacting the framework which prohibits the trafficking of persons within Nepal and across borders. Yet, because of the dangerous nature of the trafficking business, those with information about victims or perpetrators are often fearful to contact proper authorities because they are afraid for their own well-being.

But, for all of these anti–human trafficking acts and laws that have been created, the situation has changed very little. After two weeks traveling in Nepal conducting fieldwork on peace building in a post-conflict society, one glaring issue was the enormous gap between top-level institutions and those at the grassroots. While many grassroots organizations are working to end human trafficking, without support from the government, it may be a futile effort.

The Women's Rehabilitation Centre (WOREC) in Kathmandu uses anti-trafficking campaigns as a part of women's health rights initiative. The campaign provides medical support (a rarity in Nepal), psychological support, need-based support, trainings at the grassroots level, and documentation of cases of violence against women. When asked if these campaigns have decreased the number of trafficking cases, it was explained that although there has been an increase because more women are documenting their cases, this does not mean that there has been a rise in the number of trafficking cases, per se. The fact that these women are coming forward is monumental. In Nepali culture, the stigma of rape makes it extremely difficult for a woman who has been raped or violated to return to her village and reintegrate into society.

The Educated Are Most Vulnerable

At the Rural Development Centre in the district of Bara in southern Nepal, I asked if the high dropout rate among Nepali girls makes them more of a target for human trafficking. I was told that it is girls who have more education and are seeking jobs who tend to be more vulnerable. They go out of their village and out of Nepal, in search of work, which often entangles them in domestic servitude or sexual slavery. They also told me that girls from the tribal Madhesi group, who tend to be less educated, are inclined to be more homebound and not looking for a way out and therefore are less likely to fall victim to human trafficking.

In Bhairahawa, a city bordering India, we spoke with the superintendent of police. He stated that this was one of the worst areas for "human smuggling" due to the close proximity to India. He explained that even when the crime of trafficking occurs across the border, they can still investigate. However, in order to take the perpetrator into custody, a special agreement must be signed with India to prove the case is strictly criminal. This is apparently very difficult to achieve.

An NGO [nongovernmental organization] called Saathi, located in the border city of Nepalgunj, runs a 25-bed shelter where women who are shunned from their communities can stay after becoming a victim of trafficking. During our meeting on the 19th of January 2012, they reported already having ten cases of human trafficking that month. The victims are mainly uneducated, poor girls and boys from the Hill region. Their representative explained that sometimes parents "sell" their children willingly when times are difficult so the child can earn money for the family, or when they think it will be an opportunity for their child to have a better life. She estimated that around 40 percent of trafficking victims go willingly with a trafficker with the promise of work. When asked if there was any way to stop people from going abroad for work in countries known for slavery, it was explained that people would still go abroad because of economic and social problems in Nepal. Also since India and Nepal have an open border policy, human smuggling along the border is significantly easier.

Saathi spreads awareness about this issue via radio and newspapers and by having representatives travel extensively through the villages explaining their anti–human trafficking/domestic violence campaigns, providing trainings, and working closely with all village development committees.

Barriers to Ending Trafficking

Back in Kathmandu, we met with a representative of Maiti Nepal, an organization similar to Saathi, which has assisted nearly 15,000 victims of trafficking. They also provide care for children who have been trafficked or whose mothers have been trafficking victims. Because of their growing status among the international community, Maiti is able to rescue girls from Indian brothels upon petition from their parents. Sadly, 38 percent of those trafficked and rescued are HIV positive.. The representative stated that the government is working to increase laws regarding human trafficking, but thus far, only about 600 traffickers have been prosecuted or convicted. This is due in part to bribery and corruption that exists within the government and the police force. The legal process is also severely hindered by political agendas, instability, and impunity.

Clearly, human trafficking is a major issue that complicates the Nepalis' fight to rebuild their country, form a stable government, and find a sense of structure in this post-conflict period. However, between Nepal's open border policy with India, the glaring gap and utter lack of communication between government and the local level, and the impunity, lack of rule of law and unstable nature of the country, the struggle to eliminate human trafficking in Nepal is proving to be a difficult one. Nevertheless, it is inspiring to see the incredible hard work being done by extremely motivated and passionate people at the grassroots level and one can only hope that one day very soon their efforts will pay off.

VIEWPOINT 4

> *"If the immigrants had a legal path to entry, if they did not have to cross the border unlawfully, the traffickers would be naked without human crowds to hide in."*

Secure the US-Mexico Border: Open It

John Lee

John Lee is an administrator of the Open Borders website. In the following viewpoint, he argues that the US-Mexican border is dangerous and unsecure because of efforts to keep good-faith immigrants out. Many people cross the border to look for work. These people, he says, should have a way to work in the United States legally. Until a working visa program is in place, the number of immigrants entering the United States will overwhelm border security, making it difficult to find and arrest those engaged in drug smuggling or human trafficking. To secure the border, Lee concludes, the border must be opened to good-faith immigrants.

John Lee, "Secure the US-Mexico Border: Open It," Open Borders, February 25, 2013.

As you read, consider the following questions:

1. What sort of stories does the Associated Press cover in one breath, according to Lee?
2. How did travel across the border from Brownsville to Matamoros used to be regulated, according to Tony Garza?
3. What does Sheriff Lupe Trevino say is the first thing that needs to be accomplished before securing the border?

The Associated Press has a great story out on what a "secure" US-Mexico border would look like. It covers perspectives from various stakeholders on border security, with opinions running the gamut from "The border is as secure as it can ever be" to "It's obviously incredibly unsafe." I am not sure if the AP is fairly representing opinions on the border issue, but the reporting of how life on the border has evolved over time is fascinating.

One thing that strikes me in this reporting is how casually drug smugglers/slave traffickers and good-faith immigrants are easily conflated. Is a secure border one where people who want to move contraband goods or human slaves illegally cannot easily enter? Or is it one where well-meaning people can be indefinitely kept at bay for an arbitrary accident of birth? This passage juxtaposes the two quite different situations:

> And nearly all of more than 70 drug smuggling tunnels found along the border since October 2008 have been discovered in the clay-like soil of San Diego and Tijuana, some complete with hydraulic lifts and rail cars. They've produced some of the largest marijuana seizures in U.S. history.
>
> Still, few attempt to cross what was once the nation's busiest corridor for illegal immigration. As he waited for breakfast at a Tijuana migrant shelter, Jose de Jesus Scott nodded to-

> ward a roommate who did. He was caught within seconds and badly injured his legs jumping the fence.
>
> Scott, who crossed the border with relative ease until 2006, said he and a cousin tried a three-day mountain trek to San Diego in January and were caught twice. Scott, 31, was tempted to return to his wife and two young daughters near Guadalajara. But, with deep roots in suburban Los Angeles and cooking jobs that pay up to $1,200 a week, he will likely try the same route a third time.

The main thing that strikes me about the previously "unsecure" border near San Diego is that border patrol agents were overwhelmed by a mass of people until more staff and walls were brought to bear. But these masses of people almost certainly were comprised in large part, if not near entirely, of good-faith immigrants. Smugglers and traffickers merely take advantage of the confusion to sneak in with the immigrants. If the immigrants had a legal path to entry, if they did not have to cross the border unlawfully, the traffickers would be naked without human crowds to hide in. If border security advocates just want to reduce illegal trafficking, demanding "border security" before loosening immigration controls may well be putting the cart before the horse.

Even so, as I've said before, the physical reality of a long border means that human movement across it can never be fully controlled. Demanding totalitarian control as "true border security" is about as unrealistic as, if not even more so than, an open borders advocate demanding the abolition of the nation-state.

The AP covers some damning stories of peaceful Americans murdered by drug traffickers in the same breath as it covers someone trying to get to a job in suburban LA. Even if one insists that murdering smugglers and restaurant cooks should be treated identically on account of being born Mexican, it is difficult to see how one can demand that the US border patrol prioritize detaining them both equally. Yet as long as US visa policy makes it near impossible for most good-faith Mexicans who can find work in the US to do so, the reality of the border means that thousands of Mexicans just looking to work will risk their lives crossing the border, alongside smugglers and murderers.

The more reasonable policy has to be one that will allow US border patrol to focus on catching the most egregious criminals. That means giving the good-faith immigrants a legal channel to enter the US on a reasonable timeframe, reducing the flow of unlawful border crossings. This is not just my opinion, but that of even a former (Republican) US ambassador to Mexico (emphasis added):

> Tony Garza remembers watching the flow of pedestrian traffic between Brownsville and Matamoros from his father's filling station just steps from the international bridge. He recalls migrant workers crossing the fairway on the 11th hole of a golf course—northbound in the morning, southbound in the afternoon. And *during an annual celebration between the sister cities, no one was asked for their papers at the bridge. People were just expected to go home.*
>
> Garza, a Republican who served as the U.S. ambassador to Mexico from 2002 to 2009, said it's easy to become nostalgic for those times, but he reminds himself that he grew up in a border town of fewer than 50,000 people that has grown into a city of more than 200,000.
>
> The border here is more secure for the massive investment in recent years but feels less safe because the crime has changed, he said. Some of that has to do with transnational criminal organizations in Mexico and some of it is just the crime of a larger city.
>
> *Reform, he said, "would allow you to focus your resources on those activities that truly make the border less safe today."*

It's the view of those sheriffs who places themselves in harm's way to fight those murderers and smugglers (emphasis added):

Mexican Immigration

Among the hundreds of thousands of people who cross surreptitiously into the United States each year, Mexicans enjoy the distinction of being the only ones whose nationality is mentioned by name in official documents. All the rest, no matter where in the world they hail from, are lumped into the unglamorous category of "Other than Mexicans," or "OTMs" in Border Patrol parlance.

The reason is obvious: Mexicans make up about 93 percent of those surreptitious border crossers. Anyone picking up this book is surely well aware that migration from Mexico is, and has long been, a "hot button issue." Immigration in general has always been irresistible to demagogues, for it involves, or is perceived to involve, vital matters such as race and ethnicity, nationality, national security, language, culture, economics, health, law, and community. Those whose personal or political interests are served by igniting fear and hatred have always found immigrants to be convenient targets. Anti-immigrant activists condemn immigrants as strangers among us, inscrutable "others" invading our safe, comfortable, homogeneous spaces, burdening budgets, spreading crime and disease, refusing to learn "our language" or to practice "our ways."

Timothy J. Henderson, Beyond Borders: A History of Mexican Migration to the United States. *Malden, MA: Wiley-Blackwell, 2011.*

Hidalgo County sheriff Lupe Trevino points out that drug, gun and human smuggling is nothing new to the border. The difference is the attention that the drug-related violence in Mexico has drawn to the region in recent years.

> He insists his county, which includes McAllen, is safe. The crime rate is falling, and illegal immigrants account for small numbers in his jail. But asked if the border is "secure," Trevino doesn't hesitate. "Absolutely not."
>
> "When you're busting human trafficking stash houses with 60 to 100 people that are stashed in a two-, three-bedroom home for weeks at a time, how can you say you've secured the border?" he said.
>
> Trevino's view, however, is that *those people might not be there if they had a legal path to work in the U.S.*
>
> *"Immigration reform is the first thing we have to accomplish* before *we can say that we have secured the border,"* he said.
>
> In Nogales, Sheriff Tony Estrada has a unique perspective on both border security and more comprehensive immigration reform. Born in Nogales, Mexico, Estrada grew up in Nogales, Ariz., after migrating to the U.S. with his parents. He has served as a lawman in the community since 1966.
>
> He blames border security issues not only on the cartels but on the American demand for drugs. Until that wanes, he said, nothing will change. And securing the border, he added, must be a constant, ever-changing effort that blends security and political support—because the effort will never end.
>
> "The drugs are going to keep coming. The people are going to keep coming. The only thing you can do is contain it as much as possible.
>
> *"I say the border is as safe and secure as it can be, but I think people are asking for us to seal the border, and that's unrealistic,"* he said.
>
> Asked why, he said simply: "That's the nature of the border."

Simply put, if you want a secure US-Mexico border, one where law enforcement can focus on rooting out murderers and smugglers, you need open borders. You need a visa regime that lets those looking to feed their families and looking for a better life to enter legally, with a minimum of muss and fuss. When only those who cross the border unlawfully are those who have no good business being in the US, then you can have a secure border.

Periodical and Internet Sources Bibliography

The following articles have been selected to supplement the diverse views presented in this chapter.

Stephan Bauman "Immigration Reform Will Deter Human Trafficking, Not Increase It," *Christian Post*, November 8, 2013.

Denise Brennan "Migrants at Risk: How U.S. Policies Facilitate Human Trafficking," *Dissent*, March 24, 2014.

Dana Bruxvoort "Immigration Controls: Protecting Borders to End Trafficking?," Human Trafficking Center, May 14, 2015.

Tom Cohen "Unintended Consequences: 2008 Anti-Trafficking Law Contributes to Border Crisis," CNN, July 16, 2014.

Ashton Ellis "On Immigration Crisis, Obama, Not Bush, Is to Blame," *Federalist*, July 16, 2014.

Jon Feere "Trafficking Law Largely Inapplicable to Border Crisis," *The Hill*, July 24, 2014.

Fox News Latino "Porous Mexican Border Allows Alarming Trend in Human Trafficking into US," October 1, 2012.

Carl Hulse "Immigrant Surge Rooted in Law to Curb Child Trafficking," *New York Times*, July 7, 2014.

Sadhbh Walshe "Stop Allowing the Wealthy to Treat Undocumented Immigrants Like Slaves," *Guardian*, March 13, 2013.

Tiffany Williams "Human Trafficking and Immigration: The Ties That Bind," Institute for Policy Studies, January 10, 2013.

For Further Discussion

Chapter 1

1. Americans for Democracy and Human Rights in Bahrain (ADHRB) makes several policy recommendations aimed at eliminating human rights violations, including slavery and human trafficking, in Bahrain, Saudi Arabia, and Qatar. The ADHRB divides its recommendations among four specific groups: Gulf authorities, governments of source countries, the government of the United States, and the international community. Of these, which do you think has the strongest chance of effecting change in Bahrain, Saudi Arabia, and Qatar? Which has the weakest chance? Explain your choices.
2. Caitlin Seandel argues that "prison labor is the new slave labor." What are some of the similarities she mentions between historical slave labor and modern-day slave labor in prisons? Do you agree with her argument? Why, or why not?

Chapter 2

1. Erin Weaver argues that sex trafficking is a worldwide problem, with six hundred thousand to eight hundred thousand people trafficked across the US border, half of these being children. How does Maggie McNeill refute that claim? Why do you think such a discrepancy exists when it comes to calculating the number of those involved in sex trafficking? Explain.
2. IRIN argues that in Southeast Asia part of the blame for sex trafficking lies with the local government. Why does IRIN think this is so? What are some practices the local government can put in place to reduce or eliminate the risk of human trafficking?

3. Lane Anderson addresses the problem of sex trafficking during the Super Bowl, estimating that thousands of prostitutes, many of them trafficking victims, are hauled into the city hosting the yearly event. Susan Elizabeth Shepard argues that sex trafficking does not spike at the Super Bowl and that myths surrounding this issue are distracting from real issues of trafficking. With which author do you agree, and why? Cite text from the viewpoints to support your answer.

Chapter 3

1. Matthias Lehmann and Sonja Dolinsek address Germany's prostitution law that allows sex work to be viewed as a legitimate form of labor. What do you think of this law? Do you think that sex work should be viewed as a legal form of income and taxed accordingly? Do you think such a law would pass in the United States? Explain your reasoning.
2. After reading the viewpoints by Michelle Madden Dempsey and May-Len Skilbrei and Charlotta Holmström regarding the Nordic model, which criminalizes the purchase of sex rather than the people offering sexual services, do you think the United States should adopt the Nordic model? Explain, citing text from the viewpoints to support your answer.
3. New York State chief judge Jonathan Lippman argues that an initiative in New York's court system that connects those arrested for prostitution to counseling and social services in lieu of jail time is a significant shift in the way prostitution is viewed by the justice system and communities. Do you think sex trafficking courts will have an impact on trafficked individuals and will break the cycle of exploitation and arrest? Explain your reasoning.

Chapter 4

1. Denise Brennan argues that the public's understanding of trafficking is narrowly defined to mean only those kidnapped and sexually exploited; it does not include the exploitation of migrant workers who toil under abusive conditions and fear of deportation. Do you agree with Brennan's argument? Why, or why not?
2. Lauren Renda argues that the open border between Nepal and India is partly to blame for Nepal's struggle with human trafficking. Do you think that if Nepal and India instituted stricter border controls that human trafficking in the region would decrease? Why, or why not?
3. John Lee argues that open borders between the United States and Mexico would reduce human trafficking. He says that by establishing a visa regime to give immigrants who want to work a legal channel to enter the United States, there will be a reduction in the flow of unlawful border crossings and human smugglings. Do you think an open border policy between the United States and Mexico would reduce human trafficking? Explain your reasoning.

Organizations to Contact

The editors have compiled the following list of organizations concerned with the issues debated in this book. The descriptions are derived from materials provided by the organizations. All have publications or information available for interested readers. The list was compiled on the date of publication of the present volume; the information provided here may change. Be aware that many organizations take several weeks or longer to respond to inquiries, so allow as much time as possible.

Coalition Against Trafficking in Women (CATW)
PO Box 7160, JAF Station, New York, NY 10116
(212) 643-9895
e-mail: info@catwinternational.org
website: www.catwinternational.org

The Coalition Against Trafficking in Women (CATW) is a nongovernmental organization that advocates for the human rights of women and promotes policies that fight the sexual exploitation and sex trafficking of women and children around the world. CATW works to combat forced prostitution and pornography as well as sex tourism and the practice of mail-order marriages. CATW engages in ongoing projects and campaigns to end human trafficking by focusing on prevention, education, gender equality, and legislation. The CATW website offers access to fact sheets, congressional testimony, articles, press releases, videos, and reports such as "Sex Trafficking of Women in the United States: International and Domestic Trends."

Coalition to Abolish Slavery and Trafficking (CAST)
5042 Wilshire Boulevard #586, Los Angeles, CA 90036
(213) 365-1906 • fax: (213) 365-5257
e-mail: info@castla.org
website: www.castla.org

Established in 1998, the Coalition to Abolish Slavery and Trafficking (CAST) is a nonprofit organization that provides assistance to the victims of human trafficking and forced labor around the world. CAST established the first shelter in the nation dedicated solely to serving victims of trafficking and opened a family clinic dedicated to addressing the health and mental health needs of trafficking victims in the Los Angeles area. Through broad community outreach on local, state, national, and international levels, CAST brings the issue of trafficking to the forefront so that more victims will be free and empowered. Its website provides survivor stories, articles, press releases, issue papers, reports, and links to other resources on the topic.

Equality Now
PO Box 20646, Columbus Circle Station
New York, NY 10023
(212) 586-0906 • fax: (212) 586-1611
e-mail: info@equalitynow.org
website: www.equalitynow.org

Since its inception in 1992, Equality Now has worked to protect and promote the human rights of women and girls around the world. It documents violence and discrimination against women in a variety of contexts and coordinates with other human rights groups and activists to address these issues. Its areas of focus include discrimination in law, sexual violence, female genital mutilation (FGM), and human trafficking. Through grassroots activism along with international, regional, and national legal advocacy, Equality Now fights for a world in which women and men have equal rights under the law and enjoy those rights fully. Its website provides news articles, reports, fact sheets, videos, and press releases.

Free the Slaves (FTS)
1320 Nineteenth Street NW, Suite 600
Washington, DC 20036
(202) 775-7480 • fax: (202) 775-7485
e-mail: info@freetheslaves.net
website: www.freetheslaves.net

Free the Slaves (FTS) is an international nongovernmental organization working to end slavery worldwide. The group believes that economic opportunities, health services, universal education, and a strong rule of law reduce the vulnerability of impoverished people to become enslaved. FTS works to eradicate slavery by providing training, technical assistance, and grants to strengthen local organizations and agencies; educating and organizing vulnerable communities; increasing access to basic services; providing legal protection and liberation; and reducing survivor vulnerability. FTS publishes a quarterly newsletter, and its website offers access to *The FTS Blog* as well as fact sheets, backgrounders reports, policy papers, and videos, including "What Does Slavery Look Like Today?"

Human Rights First
75 Broad Street, 31st Floor, New York, NY 10004
(212) 845-5200 • fax: (212) 845-5299
website: www.humanrightsfirst.org

Human Rights First is a nonprofit international organization that advances human rights around the world. Through research and reporting on human rights abuses, advocacy for victims, and coordination with other human rights organizations, the group works to promote and protect human dignity and the rights and freedom of people everywhere. One of the group's topics of interest is human trafficking, and it is leading a campaign urging the US government and business leaders to end modern-day slavery. It published an action plan, "How to Disrupt the Business of Human Trafficking," which is available on its website, along with congressional testimony, press releases, videos, news reports, and articles such as "From Mexico to Malaysia: The U.S. Should Leverage Trade Against Trafficking."

Human Rights Watch (HRW)
350 Fifth Avenue, 34th Floor, New York, NY 10118
(212) 290-4700 • fax: (212) 736-1300
e-mail: hrwpress@hrw.org
website: www.hrw.org

Since its founding in 1978, Human Rights Watch (HRW) has worked on the international level to ensure and protect human rights for all people worldwide. HRW seeks to ensure that those who commit human rights abuses are held accountable for their actions. Often working in difficult situations—including those controlled by oppressive and tyrannical governments—HRW strives to provide accurate and impartial reporting on human rights conditions for media outlets, financial institutions, and international organizations. Videos, reports, and articles, such as "Human Trafficking: It's Not Just About Sexual Exploitation" and "The Hidden Victims of Human Trafficking," can be found on the HRW website.

Polaris Project
PO Box 65323, Washington, DC 20035
(202) 745-1001 • fax: (202) 745-1119
e-mail: info@polarisproject.org
website: www.polarisproject.org

The Polaris Project is a nonprofit organization working to eradicate all forms of human trafficking and modern-day slavery. From working with government leaders to protect victims' rights to building partnerships with the world's leading technology corporations, Polaris seeks to establish long-term change that focuses communities on identifying, reporting, and eliminating trafficking networks. The group operates the National Human Trafficking Resource Center hotline and offers a texting shortcode, BeFree (233733), to help victims of human trafficking find safety. The Polaris website features news updates, videos, fact sheets, and links to helpful resources.

Shared Hope International
PO Box 65337, Vancouver, WA 98665
(866) 437-5433
website: www.sharedhope.org

Since it was created in 1998, the nonprofit organization Shared Hope International has worked to eradicate sex trafficking of women and children. The group has three main missions: create public awareness about the crime to better prevent it; rescue women and children from sexual slavery and restore them to a safe and supportive environment; and bring justice to victims by prosecuting perpetrators. Its website offers articles, press releases, fact sheets, speech transcripts, and videos. Shared Hope publishes the reports "JuST (Juvenile Sex Trafficking) Response State System Mapping Report" and "2014 Protected Innocence Challenge: State Report Cards on the Legal Framework of Protection for the Nation's Children," which are available on its website.

Stop the Traffik

First Floor Millbank Tower, 21–24 Millbank
London SW1P 4QP
United Kingdom
(+44) (0)207 921 4258
e-mail: info@stopthetraffik.org
website: www.stopthetraffik.org

Founded in 2006, Stop the Traffik is an international coalition of human rights groups, communities, and activists working to eliminate the practice of human trafficking. To accomplish this goal, it educates policy makers and individuals on the crime; advocates for strong and effective laws against the practice and the full implementation of anti-trafficking laws that already exist; and helps victims of trafficking. The Take Action section of its website provides information on the numerous campaigns undertaken by the organization, including campaigns against the chocolate, textile, and tea industries, which are known to traffic children and young women to produce their products. Its website also offers articles, press releases, reports, and a blog, with entries such as "Change Is Happening in the Chocolate Industry" and "The Ugly Side of Fashion."

United Nations Office on Drugs and Crime (UNODC)

Vienna International Centre, Wagramer Strasse 5
Vienna A 1400
Austria

(+43) (1) 26060
e-mail: info@unodc.org
website: www.unodc.org

The United Nations Office on Drugs and Crime (UNODC) is the agency tasked with fighting illicit drugs and international crime, including human trafficking. UNODC follows the Convention Against Transnational Organized Crime and Its Protocols, an important instrument to fight international crime. The UNODC provides on its website the latest news on its efforts to combat human trafficking globally. The UNODC publishes a range of literature on the subject of human trafficking, including the "2014 Global Report on Trafficking in Persons," as well as assessment toolkits, issue papers, and international frameworks. The UNODC recently developed an online database to collect and disseminate information on human trafficking prosecutions and convictions from around the world.

Vital Voices Global Partnership
1625 Massachusetts Avenue NW, Suite 300
Washington, DC 20036
(202) 861-2625
e-mail: info@vitalvoices.org
website: www.vitalvoices.org

Founded in 1999 by First Lady Hillary Clinton and Secretary of State Madeleine Albright among others, Vital Voices Global Partnership is a nongovernmental organization focused on empowering women around the world. Vital Voices aims to help create generations of independent, self-sufficient, and productive women who will enhance their communities and provide opportunities for other women in an effort to curb human trafficking, which disproportionately affects impoverished women and young girls. The Vital Voices website offers information on the latest global initiatives to aid women and features a blog that covers news and human trafficking issues, including entries such as "Girl Power: Empowering Through Sport" and "Human Trafficking: No 'Perfect' Victim."

Bibliography of Books

Kevin Bales	*Disposable People: New Slavery in the Global Economy*. 3rd ed. Los Angeles: University of California Press, 2012.
Kevin Bales and Ron Soodalter	*The Slave Next Door: Human Trafficking and Slavery in America Today*. 2nd ed. Los Angeles: University of California Press, 2010.
Edward E. Baptist	*The Half Has Never Been Told: Slavery and the Making of American Capitalism*. New York: Basic Books, 2014.
Nita Belles	*In Our Backyard: Human Trafficking in America and What We Can Do to Stop It*. Grand Rapids, MI: Baker Books, 2015.
Denise Brennan	*Life Interrupted: Trafficking into Forced Labor in the United States*. Durham, NC: Duke University Press, 2014.
Alison Brysk and Austin Choi-Fitzpatrick, eds.	*From Human Trafficking to Human Rights: Reframing Contemporary Slavery*. Philadelphia: University of Pennsylvania Press, 2012.
Mary C. Burke	*Human Trafficking: Interdisciplinary Perspectives*. New York: Routledge, 2013.
Lydia Cacho	*Slavery Inc.: The Untold Story of International Sex Trafficking*. Berkeley, CA: Soft Skull Press, 2014.

Jessica Elliott — *The Role of Consent in Human Trafficking*. New York: Routledge, 2014.

Theresa Flores with PeggySue Wells — *The Slave Across the Street*. Boise, ID: Ampelon Publishing, 2010.

Anne T. Gallagher — *The International Law of Human Trafficking*. New York: Cambridge University Press, 2010.

Melissa Gira Grant — *Playing the Whore: The Work of Sex Work*. Brooklyn, NY: Verso, 2014.

Shyima Hall — *Hidden Girl: The True Story of a Modern-Day Child Slave*. New York: Simon & Schuster, 2015.

Stephanie Hepburn and Rita J. Simon — *Human Trafficking Around the World: Hidden in Plain Sight*. New York: Columbia University, 2013.

Kimberly Kay Hoang and Rhacel Salazar Parreñas — *Human Trafficking Reconsidered: Rethinking the Problem, Envisioning New Solutions*. Brussels, Belgium: International Debate Education Association, 2014.

Alisa Jordheim — *Made in the U.S.A.: The Sex Trafficking of America's Children*. Oviedo, FL: HigherLife Publishing, 2014.

Siddharth Kara — *Sex Trafficking: Inside the Business of Modern Slavery*. New York: Columbia University Press, 2010.

David Kyle and Rey Koslowski, eds.	*Global Human Smuggling: Comparative Perspectives.* Baltimore, MD: Johns Hopkins University Press, 2011.
Min Liu	*Migration, Prostitution, and Human Trafficking: The Voice of Chinese Women.* New Brunswick, NJ: Transaction, 2011.
Rachel Lloyd	*Girls Like Us: Fighting for a World Where Girls Are Not for Sale.* New York: HarperCollins, 2011.
Shayne Moore and Kimberly McOwen Yim	*Refuse to Do Nothing: Finding Your Power to Abolish Modern-Day Slavery.* Downers Grove, IL: InterVarsity Press, 2013.
Harold J. Newton, ed.	*Human Trafficking: Scope and Response Efforts.* New York: Nova Science, 2012.
Shiro Okubo and Louise Shelley, eds.	*Human Security, Transnational Crime and Human Trafficking: Asian and Western Perspectives.* New York: Routledge, 2011.
Michael J. Palmiotto, ed.	*Combating Human Trafficking: A Multidisciplinary Approach.* Boca Raton, FL: CRC Press, 2014.
Joel Quirk	*The Anti-Slavery Project: From the Slave Trade to Human Trafficking.* Philadelphia: University of Pennsylvania Press, 2011.

Louise Shelley	*Human Trafficking: A Global Perspective.* New York: Cambridge University Press, 2010.
Julian Sher	*Somebody's Daughter: The Hidden Story of America's Prostituted Children and the Battle to Save Them.* Chicago, IL: Chicago Review Press, 2013.
Holly Austin Smith	*Walking Prey: How America's Youth Are Vulnerable to Sex Slavery.* New York: Palgrave Macmillan, 2014.
Leonard Territo and Nataliya Glover	*Criminal Investigation of Sex Trafficking in America.* Boca Raton, FL: CRC Press, 2013.
Daniel Walker	*God in a Brothel: An Undercover Journey into Sex Trafficking and Rescue.* Downers Grove, IL: InterVarsity Press, 2011.
John Winterdyk, Benjamin Perrin, and Philip Reichel, eds.	*Human Trafficking: Exploring the International Nature, Concerns, and Complexities.* Boca Raton, FL: CRC Press, 2012.

Index

C

D

E

F

G

H

K

L

M

N

O

P

Q

R

S

T

U

V

W

X

Y

CPSIA information can be obtained
at www.ICGtesting.com
Printed in the USA
FFOW05n0955160116